NEW MEXICO HEROINES OF THE TWENTIETH CENTURY

NEW MEXICO HEROINES OF THE TWENTIETH CENTURY

Role Models for Today

Ron Hamm, PhD

Santa Fe

Sunstone books may be purchased for educational, business, or sales promotional use.
For information please write: Special Markets Department, Sunstone Press,
P.O. Box 2321, Santa Fe, New Mexico 87504-2321.

eBook 978-1-61139-630-0

Library of Congress Cataloging-in-Publication Data

Names: Hamm, Ron, 1935- author.
Title: New Mexico heroines of the twentieth century : role models for today / Ron Hamm.
Description: Santa Fe, New Mexico : Sunstone Press, [2022] | Includes bibliographical references and index. | Summary: "An account of women who have left their mark on New Mexico"-- Provided by publisher.
Identifiers: LCCN 2021054661 | ISBN 9781632933768 (paperback) | ISBN 9781611396300 (epub) | ISBN 1632933768 (paperback)
Subjects: LCSH: Women--New Mexico--History--Biography--20th century. | Role models--Women--New Mexico--Biography. | LCGFT: Biographies.
Classification: LCC HQ1154 .H226 2021 | DDC 920.72--dc23/eng/20211109
LC record available at https://lccn.loc.gov/2021054661

WWW.SUNSTONEPRESS.COM
SUNSTONE PRESS / POST OFFICE BOX 2321 / SANTA FE, NM 87504-2321 /USA
(505) 988-4418

For Drewey Wayne Gunn 1939–2018

CONTENTS

INTRODUCTION

For the girls and young women of New Mexico. Look to your foremothers.

For a century, New Mexico women of diverse ethnicities, backgrounds, and beliefs have distinguished themselves in wide-ranging fields of interest and attainment. Their accomplishments and contributions have been truly staggering. There have been some attempts by others to write of some them, but this book aspires to a more ambitious goal by looking at New Mexico's extraordinary women of the entire twentieth century.

Why this book? Why now? The short answer is that such a book hasn't been written. Aspects of it have been broached more than two dozen times in the past thirty-five years. None has approached the subject in the way this book does, i.e., to record, assess, demonstrate, and praise the role New Mexico women of the twentieth century have played and continue to play in forging New Mexico into the vibrant place that it is. There has been a glaring lack of recognition for these women in scholarly writing, the media, and on the speaker's platform. Martha Shipman Andrews in *Out of the Shadows* has observed that "Book-length, scholarly studies of New Mexico women...from frontier times down to the present are poorly represented in the wider historiography of New Mexico."

It might be worthwhile to share some insights about how this book came together and to point out what it is and what it is not. First of all, it contains limited original material, almost none. In some cases, I have made reference to my books and articles. I have relied heavily on secondary sources and have made liberal use of the Doctrine of Fair Use that permits limited use of material without having permission from the copyright holder so long as proper attribution is provided. I have always attempted to do so. I have also attempted to heed my publisher's stricture to allow the subject to speak for herself wherever possible. Again, that has not always been achieved, especially when a subject has left no record of her writings. If my subject has not written of her life, I have turned to a qualified commentator, often more than one.

This has not been an easy book to write. But not for the usual reasons such as writer's block or lack of material. Rather, it has been to the contrary—too many subjects or too much material to wade through and to evaluate. Sift. Sift. Sift. Every time I thought I was finished, a name led me to another or to another source of multiple names. And my reading list seemed never to stop growing. I still have many more sources I would like to read. One of the conventions I have adopted is to include birth and death dates when available. If this information is missing, it is because I could not locate it. Very few names of husbands are included unless such information was relevant. This is a book about women, not men. Another custom I have attempted to follow is to use the surname preferred by the woman herself or how she was customarily known. This is my usage even though she might be married.

Who is in; who is out? Some women, in my judgment, had a more lasting impact than others. My admitted biases for inclusion have been toward writers and artists—women I admire for their creativity or contribution to our society. Close behind are political activists. Many of them were suffragists. Entertainers and performers, not so much. Often my subjects have been written of previously. Sometimes even a biography exists; that is the case for many of them. Almost all of my subjects deserve a deeper dive than I was able to provide. And undoubtedly there are still more sources to be consulted.

It is always hard to begin. I wrestled with the parameters of inclusion. Finally, I made a couple of decisions: first, it was my book and therefore I got to set the rules; and, second, I should begin unrestrained by firm protocols. It was easy. I just began. The number of subjects began to accumulate. Someone else might have done things differently. But lassitude struck. I couldn't face the computer. I stopped for two long months. Finally I began again with a new focus and a new set of criteria.

Here it is and it made all the difference.

This book surveys women who lived heroic lives in twentieth century New Mexico. It looks at a diverse group of women noted for their leadership, contributions, achievements, and courage. Many but not all of of them came from the fields of medicine and public service. It is hoped this book will hold these women up as role models for emulation by today's New Mexico girls and young women, no matter their background, heritage, or beliefs.

Voila!

I suddenly remembered what my doctoral dissertation advisor admonished and what I myself told freshman essay writers: to focus. That I could not write about the whole world. That I had to limit my material and funnel it until I could get my arms around the subject. I did. The result was amazing. But the result was a complete rewrite.

A writing project is never easy. I do not use outlines in approaching a new book. But I do employ a device I find useful: early on formulating a working title. Even if the title changes over the course of months or maybe a year (and this one did), it continues to serve as a guiding principle. I often find that a title serves as a kind of thesis statement and helps me get my arms around the project and to see the larger picture. Here is an example. An earlier book of mine traced four generations of a New Mexico banking/ranching/political family. I quickly settled on the title, *Bursums of New Mexico: Four Generations of Leadership and Service*. The rest flowed. I discovered that topic was exactly what I was writing about. This book was originally titled *Mothers, Lovers, & Others: 400 Years of New Mexico Women Who Made a Difference*. But it was an entirely different book. There are some common threads in that book and this.

As an aid to the reader, I include an appendix that identifies what these women did throughout their lives, both as a vocation and an avocation. Their fields of work include art, literature, social and political activism–especially suffrage– politics and government, science and medicine, communications, and money and banking. It quickly became obvious to me when compiling this section that a handful of fields predominate: arts and music, education and scholarship, writing, and science and medicine. A slight surprise, given that New Mexico was a largely rural state in the early part of the twentieth century with plenty of farming and ranching opportunities, is that few women were actively engaged in these pursuits. Since many of my subjects lived before they had the right to vote, suffrage was an essential cause to their minds, and they worked diligently on its behalf. And finally, there were some women of genuine physical courage: Sarah Rooke and Susie Parks, among others, who "manned" their telephone switchboards during times of great peril to their communities. Feats of courage called for new terminology. All these women were different from those who came before.

Many of the subjects in this book came to see themselves as "New Women," transformed in part by the times in which they lived—a period they viewed as more open perhaps than in the past to acceptance of women as more than mere objects to to carry on the species. They needed a new nomenclature. Elsie Clews Parsons must have been the most outstanding example. The less-known Frances Minerva Nunnery also epitomizes this ideal. The "New Woman" was a feminist ideal that emerged in the late nineteenth century and had a profound influence on feminism well into the twentieth century. The transformation was accompanied for some by their move to the Southwest. So it was for Natalie Curtis, featured in Lesley Poling-Kempes's *Ladies of the Canyons,* which was so helpful to me in the early stages of writing this book. Likewise, Alice Klauber discovered her "Santa Fe self which is a new woman" upon first stepping foot in New Mexico's capital city.

As Poling-Kempes notes, neither were these women Betty Crocker look-alikes, nor shrinking violets, nor really anything in between or outside those once prevailing norms. They set their own standards as to how they were to be seen and how they saw themselves. In brief, they were self-proclaimed "New Women," quite boldly ahead of their milieu in terms of their attitudes, outlooks, and perceptions by others by practically all prevailing measures—in thoughts, words, deeds, and actions. Their attributes were admirable. I quickly came to know and admire the women in my book and to be convinced that New Mexico has been vastly enriched by their presence. They are truly examples of lives well lived. Most of us who know anything about New Mexico are familiar with such luminaries as Georgia O'Keeffe, Willa Cather, Mary Austin, Erna Fergusson, Agnes Morley Cleaveland, and many more. On the other hand, who among us have heard of Jenny Vincent, a social activist firebrand who performed with the likes of Woody Guthrie and Pete Seeger? Or the aforementioned Frances Nunnery, shaped by adversity and illness, who succeeded at all she put her hand to. Joan Myers in *Pie Town Woman* notes that Nunnery "could well serve as a model of determination and independence for us all." By her death at age 99, she had become the exact opposite for those who mistakenly believe women are frail and powerless. Instead, she was "a determined, ingenious entrepreneur [who defied] every stereotype about women." "I've never got the hang of being old," she remarked.

One favorite is Agnes Martin, because I would like to emulate her achievements and philosophy, and perhaps her financial success as well. Martin worked into her nineties in a Taos retirement community. In doing so, she lived her credo: "We are born as verbs rather than as nouns. We are born to function in life, to work and do all positive actions that will carry out our potential..." It doesn't hurt that her paintings were selling for the millions of dollars.

Another favorite—but for different reasons because her life and outlook were exactly opposite of Martin—is Edith Warner, whose life was informed by her kindness and humility. Self-effacing and reserved, Warner was a neighbor and friend to both the brilliant scientists who developed the atomic bomb at the nearby Los Alamos National Laboratory during World War II and to her nearby Native American neighbors at San Ildefonso Pueblo. Warner saw everyone—red or white—alike. "It matters not that the color of skin be different, that language be not the same, that even the gods of our fathers be known by a different name. We are people, the same kind of human beings who live and love and go on...," she once said. My book is full of such epiphanies.

In addition to discovering how these women spent their lives, I learned that life lessons are where you find them and that a major takeaway from studying and writing about these fascinating women is that an extraordinarily large number of them lived to an exceptionally ripe old age. Therefore, I would suggest to young New Mexico women hoping to emulate their foremothers that an additional benefit of such involvement would be increased longevity. I am certain that this characteristic can be traced to their desire to better the environment—whether physical or social—in which they found themselves. Not being a gerontologist but certainly well on the road to becoming an official Old Person myself, I was pleased to learn that. Aside from the aforementioned Vincent, Martin, and Nunnery, I could reel off the names of literally dozens of women who reached their eighties, nineties, and some their early hundreds. The reason? I am convinced it was because they were engaged. Perhaps no longer in the sense that they had once become anthropologists working in the field or makers of adobe for homes, but they were doing something. They were engaged with life, friends, and their professions. They were contributing. In other words, they were working at their work. As I read and wrote, I gradually discovered some of the major themes of this book emerging: self-discovery, fortitude, and liberation.

In this context I want to share some personal anecdotes because they help to explain how I found some of my subjects. That is a question many readers ask. Some made the book on pure serendipity. At coffee one morning I casually asked a friend for suggestions. His reply? "Yeah. Maybe my ex-wife." It turns out Erica Elliott MD was a "real keeper." Among her many accomplishments after obtaining a medical degree at the University of New Mexico was treating the state's Native Americans in its rural areas. I remembered a friend telling me of a vague recollections of an ornithologist who had lived and worked in southern New Mexico. Her name was Florence Bailey, and she had rightfully earned the title of "First Lady of Ornithology." Bailey did it all in ornithology. Not only did she work with the National Audubon Society during its formative years, she is also credited with writing the first known American bird guide, Birds *Through an Opera-Glass,* published in 1890. She spent decades in the Southwest, particularly in New Mexico, and wrote two field guides for the state. In 1929 the University of New Mexico awarded her a Doctor of Laws degree for her *Birds of New Mexico*. But I dug in the library as well. My bookshelves are much fuller now with acquisitions about these women.

I have relied on the wisdom and insights of such commentators as Lesley Poling-Kempes. In *Ladies of the Canyons*, she observed that women of the early part of the twentieth century, when many of my subjects lived, had to be "independent, ambitious, stubborn, unconventional, and tenacious." These are not bad criteria for deciding on parameters for inclusion in this book. I also want to acknowledge Poling-Kemps' insights into women's contributions as exemplified in *Ladies of the Canyons* and *The Harvey Girls: Women Who Opened the West.* I am indebted to this talented researcher and writer for providing inspiration to move forward and for helping me understand their "interconnectivity."

As I pondered between including and omitting subjects. I found it nigh impossible to identify every worthy contender. I hope that in these pages the reader will make some new friends and find sources of inspiration and that she will learn more of these remarkable molders and shapers of New Mexico. I did time and again in researching and writing this book.

—Ron Hamm

PORTRAITS OF HEROINES

Sophie Bledsoe Aberle. Wikipedia.

Aberle, Sophie Bledsoe Brophy, MD, PhD. Native American anthropologist, physician, health administrator. Director of the United Pueblo Agency in 1935, Sophie Aberle lived among the Pueblo people while conducting significant anthropological and medical studies. A graduate of Stanford University and one of the first female members of its medical faculty, Aberle wrote *The Pueblo Indians of New Mexico.* As a youth she had several instrumental female mentors, among them her grandmother and namesake, Sophia Bledsoe Herrick, a science and history writer for popular magazines. Educated by private tutors, Aberle (the name was from a brief marriage) applied for and received high school credit to be admitted to the University of California in Berkeley. She later transferred to Stanford where she completed her BA in 1923, MA in 1925, and a doctorate in anatomy in 1927. Upon leaving Stanford, she came to New Mexico for the first time to research sexual behavior at San Juan Pueblo. Quickly discovering that the language barrier would prevent that, instead she focused on the social life and customs of the pueblo. She returned to school at Yale University School of Medicine where she researched female reproductive biology, earning an MD in 1930. She was one of the first women appointees of the National Science Board. (1896–1966). *Notable New Mexico Women.* Sophie Aberle Papers 1913–1987 Collection Number: MSS 509, Center for Southwest Research and Special Collections, University of New Mexico.

Barbara Freire-Marreco Aitken. Courtesy of Sunstone Press.

Aitken, Barbara Freire-Marreco. Pueblo researcher. A member of the first class of anthropology students at Oxford University where she held a prestigious research fellowship. Barbara Aitken attained remarkable command of the Tewa language and customs. Aitken specialized in studying the Santa Clara Pueblo in New Mexico. She originally considered them "uncivilized." The story of this intrepid, remarkable woman, from a proper English family and adherent to the Church of England, is told in her biography by Mary Ellen Blair. *A Life Well Led: The Biography of Barbara Freire-Marreco Aitken*. Her papers are held at the Pitt Rivers Museum at Oxford University. (1879–1967). *Daughters of the Desert.*

Allen, Paula Gunn, PhD. Native American poet, literary critic, activist, professor, novelist. Paula Gunn Allen was born on the Cubero land grant in New Mexico into Laguna, Sioux, Pueblo, and Chicano cultures. Although she held a doctorate and taught at the University of California at Berkeley, Allen was principally known for her many writings about Native American life. Among her five books of poetry are *The Blind Lion* (1974), *A Cannon Between My Knees* (1981), and *Shadow Country* (1982). Her fiction includes *The Woman Who Owns the Shadows (*1983). Her principal nonfiction publications are *The Sacred Hoop: Recovering the Feminine in American Indian Traditio*ns (1986) and *Grandmothers of the Light: A Medicine Woman's Source Book* (1991). She encouraged publication of Native American literature and educated others about it. Allen was active in the American feminist movement and its antiwar and antinuclear organizations. (1939–2008). *History is a Weapon: Who is Your Mother? Red Roots of White Feminism.*

Paula Gunn Allen.

Alvord, Lori Arviso, MD. Trailblazer in Western medicine and traditional healing. The subtitle of Lori Alvord's autobiography, *The Scalpel and the Silver Bear: The First Navajo Woman Surgeon Combines Western Medicine and Traditional Medicine,* tells the story of this remarkable Native American woman. She rose from a traditional Navajo childhood, growing up at Crownpoint, New Mexico, to obtain a bachelor's degree from Dartmouth College and then a medical education from Stanford University because her mother encouraged her "to read and to dream." Her career, which has encompassed service to her people at the Gallup Indian Medical Center,

Lori Arviso Alvord.
Astria Health.

then administrative roles guiding young Native Americans through three schools of medicine, demonstrates that, in her words, "a minority woman can travel across cultural, class, and educational borders and become a part of a medical world whose doors have been closed to minority people" for most of their existence. Dr. Alvord has learned to heal the whole person, not just to treat him or her. Incorporating some elements of Navajo beliefs in her healing is "a very strong kind of medicine" which mixes together "the best of both worlds." Her beliefs emphasize that "how you relate to everything around you" results in walking in beauty and leads to restoration of harmony—the ultimate goal of her people's healing process. Alvord continues to practice, write, and talk about what she has learned and what she wants other Native Americans to understand. (1958–). *The Scalpel and the Silver Bear: The First Navajo Woman Surgeon Combines Western Medicine and Traditional Medicine.*

Aragon, Jesusita. Midwife and natural healer. Jesusita Aragon carried on her century-long lineage of New Mexico healers into her nineties as a *partera,* or midwife, as well as a *medica,* or healer. Jesusita's first delivery was at age fourteen when she delivered her aunt's baby because her midwife grandmother had been called away. People came hundreds of miles for her services. It is believed that she delivered a majority of the babies in her home area of San Miguel County. She initially charged $10 for each delivery, gradually increasing over time, regretting that it cost so much. Jesusita originally went to people's homes on horseback. She also had a birthing center at the front of her house. At one time she had ten beds. Jesusita had a special sympathy for single mothers. At 23 years of age, she was pregnant and unmarried. When her father told her to leave the family home, she built her own house, felling trees and carrying the wood on her back. She delivered her second baby alone. During labor, Jesusita used no fetal monitor except her hands. She could feel the baby's heartbeat through the top of its head. "My babies are all over the world," she remembered." (1908–2005). *Mothering Magazine*, November 1998.

Polly Arango. New Hampshire Family Voices.

Arango, Mary Elizabeth Egan, "Polly." Children's advocate. Among Polly Arango's contributions to the well-being of American children was as Executive Director of the Family Voices network. She served on the boards of the New Mexico Voices of Children, New Mexico Development Disabilities Planning Council, New Mexico Medicaid Advisory Committee, and the Pew Commission on Children in Foster Care. She played a critical role in the formation and development of the Family-to-Family Health Information Centers. There was no national strategy to engage families when work began on health care reform in 1992. Polly produced a weekly newsletter with key ideas about children with special needs and about health care reform. She believed in the strength of all families to nurture themselves and their children and to partner in improving health care. Polly was a skilled listener who recognized that everyone's concerns were important and who also knew how to create consensus. (1942–2010). New Hampshire Family Voices.

Armer, Laura Adams. Author, photographer. Laura Adams Armer spent forty years interpreting Navajo life to young readers because she believed they "need something to dream about." Her special interest in the Navajo and the Southwest resulted in her silent film *The Mountain Chant* (1928) and photographs of day-to-day activities of the Navajo including sandpainting. She also wrote *Waterless Mountain*. From around 1900, Adams operated a business in San Francisco as a portrait photographer and displayed her works at exhibitions. (1874–1963). https://www.goodreads.com/author/show/581338.Laura_Adams_Armer.

Laura Adams Armer.

Margaret McEvoy Armer-Reid.
Ms0461_B21_F01_001, Ms0464 Guide to the Armer-Reid papers, 1884–1982,
Box 21, Folder 1,
New Mexico State University Library Archives and Special Collections.

Armer-Reid, Margaret McEvoy. New Mexico Goat Queen. Margaret Armer-Reid exhibited New Mexico Angora goats at the 1904 St. Louis World's Fair to "prove to the world that the pluck of a woman, though she be left widowed and poor, is equal to the task of achieving fortune when intelligently applied to opportunities." Armer-Reid made a great deal of money in goat raising by dint of hard work and planning. "She is the queen of the Angora ranges of the great Southwest," read contemporary accounts. When her husband died, he left her their children and her only a small herd of milk goats. The family was using the goats for its milk and meat when Armer-Reid saw another use. The goats became valuable as a source of income with textile manufacturers using more and more of the long, silken Angora fleece. Gradually, Armer-Reid began buying pedigreed goats. She was an innovator in utilizing new technology. While shearing had been done by hand, she adapted a steam-powered machine to assume the chore. Mrs. Armer-Reid wrote the *Angora Journal* which revealed her never-failing confidence in the future of her industry. (1864–1933). *The American Woman's Review*, November 1904. *Angora Journal*, January 1934. Sherry Fletcher Collection. Reproduced with permission.

Dolores Elizabeth "Lola" de Chávez de Armijo. Find A Grave. Memorial.

de Armijo, Dolores Elizabeth "Lola" de Chávez. Breaker of the New Mexico glass ceiling. In 1912, State Librarian Lola Chavez de Armijo filed a gender discrimination lawsuit after Governor W.C. McDonald sought to replace her, claiming she was unqualified to hold office under the constitution of New Mexico because of her gender. The New Mexico Supreme Court ruled in her favor, and legislation followed, allowing women to hold appointed office. Perhaps she was following in the footsteps of her father, Colonel Jose Francisco Chávez, a Civil War hero and the first Superintendent of Public Education of the Territory of New Mexico. She was originally appointed State Librarian by Governor George Curry in 1909. At age fifty-five, Doña Lola won her lawsuit and remained as State Librarian until 1917. Doña Lola was also the first Hispanic woman to hold statewide political office under a governor of the United States. She is regarded as a model of the defense of civil, labor, and political rights for Hispanics and for women in New Mexico. Her work has made it possible for women to participate much more fully in state government. (1858–1929). Note: Find A Grave says 1863–1919. New Mexico Historic Women Marker Initiative.

Julia Brown Asplund.
El Palacio.
F791P15c1Vol.30.

Asplund, Julia Brown. New Mexico's first professionally trained librarian. Julia Asplund was New Mexico's first professionally trained librarian. Asplund was interested in all social legislation. But her fifty active years in New Mexico were devoted to bringing library service to all New Mexicans. Her life exemplified a strong belief in education through books. Asplund came to Albuquerque in 1903 to organize the Territorial University's library, but two years later she and her husband moved to Santa Fe. Beginning in 1909, she surveyed school libraries for the Territorial Department of Education. Five counties reported no libraries; holdings of others ranged from one to 2,100 books. In 1929, the legislature enacted a bill to establish a state library agency, with its librarian also serving as librarian of the Museum of New Mexico. The total appropriation was $2,000. From her salary the first year Asplund spent $618 for supplies and squeezed a trifle more than $100 for books. Other books came as gifts. Somehow, she managed to circulate 2,000 books that year. Asplund also worked for women's suffrage and establishment of a girls' reform school. Asplund never wavered in her belief in equality for her gender. In 1916, she told the State Federation of Women's Clubs, "[L]et us never for a moment despair of the future of democratic institutions. Let us never give up the ideals of democracy, that democracy which is to come, which is almost here, when men and women will stand hand in hand upon the high level of personal, legal and political equality...." (1875–1958). American Association of University Women-New Mexico, "Julia Brown Asplund." 1976. https://digitalrepository.unm.edu/nm_women_aauw/1/ *Notable New Mexico Women. Women in Education: New Mexico.*

Katherine Acoya Augustine.

Augustine, Katherine Acoya. Americanization through education. Laguna Pueblo native Katherine Acoya Augustine credits professional training through nursing education for equipping her "to cope and survive" even though her Native heritage was "stripped away" in the process. Although Augustine came from a long line of teachers, she early on "set her cap on nursing," a profession she pursued for more than four decades. Her work and subsequent volunteer opportunities took her far afield from New Mexico to Siberia, Central Asia, Moscow, Lithuania, and China. (1929–unknown). *Growing Up and Looking Out: My Life from Laguna Pueblo to Albuquerque. Tales My Grandmother Told Me and Being Laguna.*

Mary Hunter Austin.

Austin, Mary Hunter Author and cultural preservationist. In *The Land of Journeys' Endings* Mary Austin wrote that "New Mexico is still a place in which the miraculous may happen," observing elsewhere that "[t]o understand the fashion of any life, one must know the land it is lived in and the procession of the year." This she did, spending many years in Santa Fe, finally settling there in her mid-50s. Through her novels, poems, plays, short stories, lectures, and espousal of social justice, Austin advocated for Hispanic and Native peoples. She did much more than write, helping establish the Santa Fe Little Theatre (still operating), and directing its first production. Austin was also active in preserving the local culture, establishing the Spanish Colonial Arts Society in 1925. She entitled her 1932 memoir *Earth Horizon*—derived from the indigenous *Rain Song* relating to the source of experience—explaining that her writing explored the search for the norm of moral and spiritual adjustment. Austin had originally come to Santa Fe to study Pueblo land laws and customs, later joining the successful fight to defeat the controversial Bursum Bill which would have stripped land from the Pueblos. (1868–1934). *Notable New Mexico Women. The Land of Journeys' Endings. Southwest Classics. This Spell of New Mexico.*

Florence Augusta Merriam Bailey. Vernon Bailey Papers.
American Heritage Center, University of Wyoming.

Bailey, Florence Augusta Merriam. First Lady of New Mexico ornithology. Florence Merriam Bailey was a nationally recognized American nature writer and ornithologist who saw birds as "winged messengers of heaven." Not only did she work with the National Audubon Society during its formative years, Bailey also contributed articles for *Audubon Magazine* while still in college. She is credited with writing the first known American bird guide which did not presuppose hunting birds as a field sport, *Birds Through an Opera Glass* (1889). Biographer Harriett Kofalk calls her "one of the most important nature writers of the nineteenth century." Bailey spent decades in the Southwest, particularly in New Mexico, and wrote field guides for the state. In 1929, the University of New Mexico awarded her an honorary law degree for *Birds of New Mexico*. In it Bailey noted that New Mexico "had the distinction" of being the first state "from which bird notes were recorded by white men." She was referring to the Coronado Expedition of 1540. Bailey herself first entered New Mexico in 1901 with her husband on birding expeditions that extended over several years. Her first book of the area, *Birds of the Western United States*, earned her the distinction of being recognized as the "only known woman naturalist working in the Southwest." She later wrote *Birds of the Lower Rio Grande Valley.* (1863–1948). *Early Women in Science. Notable New Mexico Women. Birds of New Mexico. No Woman Tenderfoot.*

Eve Ball. Courtesy of Lynda A. Sanchez.

Ball, Eve. Custodian of Apache history. Eve Ball's honesty, patience, and determination won the confidence of the Apache elders, thereby preserving oral histories that were certain to have been lost otherwise. After moving to Ruidoso in 1949 to live near the Mescalero Apache Reservation, she became a well-known author and historian of their culture. Her knowledge came from first-hand interaction with the people. She spent more than forty years interviewing Mescalero and Chiricahua Apache people throughout southern New Mexico to deepen her understanding and knowledge. Many days, she would watch tribal members walk past her home into town. It took many years for her to connect with them. Over time, the Apache began to trust her and started to share their stories. She took a leadership role in other activities, including serving as president of the New Mexico Folklore Society. Eve wrote more than one hundred fifty articles and six books. In 1984, the US Senate honored her work. (1890–1984). *Women Marked for History.* New Mexico Historic Women Marker Initiative. Lynda A. Sanchez, "Stories of Survival as told by Eve Ball." *La Crónica de Nuevo México*, October 2009.

Banks, Jeanne. STEM (science, technology, engineering, mathematics) mentor. Jeanne Banks cares about educational opportunities for young people and working women, especially in science and engineering. She pursues this passion as a member of the New Mexico Network for Women in Science and Engineering. Banks believes young women must be encouraged to pursue mathematics and science during their early schooling so they have a broader range of career choices. She also wants to serve as a role model for young women, making scientific careers more desirable for them. Banks has raised scholarship funds, supported STEM conferences, and mentored young Albuquerque women for more than three decades, As Albuquerque coordinator for the Northrop Grumman Foundation, she has helped funnel several hundred thousand dollars into the Albuquerque community. The company also conferred its Woman of Achievement Award on Banks in recognition of her accomplishments "in advancing the professional, economic, social and business presence of women in the workplace." (1954–). New Mexico Network for Women in Science and Engineering.

Florence Dibell Bartlett. Florence Dibell Bartlett at the Museum of International Folk Art on opening day, September 5, 1953. Negative no. 1469 (detail), MOIFA General Image Collection, AR.00009.3, Bartlett Library and Archives, Museum of International Folk Art.

Bartlett, Florence Dibell. Folk art collector. Florence Dibell Bartlett founded the Museum of International Folk Art in Santa Fe so it might "contribute toward greater mutual understanding among the various peoples of the world." Bartlett believed folk art would foster "an appreciation of the culture and craft of other countries" and provide "one avenue for a closer understanding between men." She believed folk art is a bond between the people of the world. The museum's holdings represent diverse cultures and constitute the largest collection of international folk art in the world, all drawing on Bartlett's major interests. Guiding the core collection of objects from thirty-four countries, Bartlett helped expand it to 130,000 objects from more than one hundred countries. (1881–1953). Museum of International Folk Art.

Benedict, Ruth, PhD. Anthropologist and folklorist. Ruth Benedict was an early student of the celebrated Elsie Clews Parsons. She was also a protégé of the noted Franz Boas. Although hampered by deafness, she carried out significant fieldwork in collecting myths and tales at Zuni and Cochiti Pueblos. Her *Patterns of Culture* is said to be the single-most popular and influential work by a twentieth century anthropologist. Her work had a strong influence on cultural anthropology. She once said, " I love to speak out the intense inspiration that comes to me from the lives of strong women." Benedict also was a poet. (1887–1948). *Daughters of the Desert.*

Ruth Benedict.

Susan Berry. Courtesy of Silver City NM Museum.

Berry, Susan M. Retired Director of the Silver City Museum and font of local history. Susan Berry continues to serve by sharing her vast knowledge of Silver City, New Mexico, and environs despite her own heavy research and writing load. She is co-author with Sharman Apt Russell of *Built to Last: An Architectural History of Silver City* and numerous articles. *True West* Magazine called her "a Silver City Treasure." Susan Berry deserves a big salute along with a host of mostly unheralded sisters (and brothers) in archives, special collections, and specialized libraries around New Mexico for their invaluable assistance to New Mexico writers. (1952–). Ron Hamm.

Alice McLellan Birney.

Birney, Alice McLellan. National "mother." Alice McLellan Birney founded and was first president of the National Congress of Mothers, organized in New Mexico in 1915. It became the National Parent-Teacher Association (PTA), which Birney co-founded. She studied medicine before pursuing a successful advertising career. Birney cared deeply about children's welfare and education, noting, "In the child and in our treatment of him rests the solution of the problems which confront the state and society today." Aiming to create a better world for children and youth by teaching their mothers about raising and educating children and about child welfare, Birney conceived the idea for the National Congress of Mothers. She helped marshal more than two thousand women for a "Mothers' Congress" in Washington, DC. From it emerged the National Congress of Mothers, which Birney led as president until 1902. The organization, which eventually became the PTA, worked to enact child labor laws, hot lunch programs, mandatory immunization, a public school health service, and kindergarten classes. Today the PTA serves more than seven million members. (1858–1907). *Women in Education: New Mexico.*

Sallie Bingham

Bingham, Sallie. Author and community and arts advocate. Born in 1937 to a newspaper-owning family in Louisville, Kentucky, Bingham left at seventeen to go to Radcliffe College, graduating with honors in English in 1958. Her first published story, "Winter Term," gave her a taste of what it took to hold out against censorship. After her first novel, *After Such Knowledge,* appeared in 1962 she went on to publish sixteen novels, collections of short stories and two memoirs and two plays, produced off-off-Broadway in the 1980s. Conflict following the sale of the Bingham companies in the late 1980s led to her move to settle in New Mexico. Inspired by the Feminist Movement, Bingham founded the Kentucky Foundation For Women which makes grants to feminist artists living in that state. She also founded The Sallie Bingham Archive for Women's History and Papers at Duke University and cofounded The Women's Project in New York City which continues to produce plays written and directed by women. She also started Santa Fe Stages. *Little Brother,* a memoir was published in April 2022. Blessed with three sons, she has also written a memoir of her youngest who died tragically. (1937–) Photograph by Camila Motta.

Bitler, Sister Mary Joaquin, SC. A mighty force: faith and healing. In 1951, Sister of Charity Mary Joaquin Bitler was called to Santa Fe as Supervisor of Nursing at Santa Fe's antiquated St. Vincent Hospital. Later, as Administrator, she was lauded for her achievements in health care and for bringing that care to the poor of New Mexico. Considered by many a brilliant businesswoman, she turned St. Vincent's into a state-of-the art facility in its time. A tough hospital administrator, she had many admirers as well as some enemies; a devout nun, she drew strength from her faith to open her heart to the poor and the sick, while she herself suffered a chronic and debilitating illness. In 1977, after succeeding in providing Santa Fe a new and greatly expanded community owned hospital, Sister Joaquin retreated to a life of contemplation and prayer in a little hermitage in central Mexico. Appalled by the poverty and sickness around her—the distended stomachs of hungry children, the heart-breaking number of infant deaths from dysentery and other parasitic diseases—she opened a small clinic to treat the villagers, most of whom had never seen a doctor or had any access to health care. Her last years were spent living as a hermit in New Mexico's Christ in the Desert Benedictine Monastery. (1911?-2003). *Charity's Sister: The Story of Sister Mary Joaquin Bitler, SC.* Sunstone Press.

Blake, Alice Alta, "Allie." The Angel of Trementina. A call to service as a Presbyterian missionary summoned Alice Alta Blake to rural northern New Mexico in 1889. It kept her there for the next forty years as her initial antipathy toward the Hispanic Catholic populace she encountered gradually turned to love and affection. That metamorphosis enabled her to find spiritual and professional fulfillment in ministering to them—first in education and later in health care and general advocacy for their well-being. The story of this strong woman of faith is told in *Women of the New Mexico Frontier 1846–1912.* Blake's epiphany is revealed in the transition from her initial characterization of the subjects of her mission as a people having moral values "so corrupt" that they would "scorch the soul of an angel" to one of "courtesy, warm-hearted and hospitable, needing only to be known to be loved ..." In turn, these people came to see her as "a mother of us all," while others regarded her as "the angel of Trementina," remembering the now-deserted tiny village where she labored on their behalf for so long. (1867–1950). *Women of the New Mexico Frontier 1846–1912.*

Maude Elizabeth McFie Bloom. RG85-125, John Porter Bloom collection, Rio Grande Historical Collections, New Mexico State University Library Archives and Special Collections.

Bloom, Maude Elizabeth McFie. Writer and ethnohistorian. Maude Elizabeth McFie Bloom knew whereof she wrote. In 1903, as a senior at New Mexico A&M College (now New Mexico State University), she did her senior thesis on those Anglo settlers who helped create the history of New Mexico's Mesilla Valley. Much of her material came directly from oral interviews with the men and women who settled various land grants in the Valley—members of the Missouri Volunteers who marched south through the valley to El Paso, bringing other men who settled there. The McFie family also was active in its history. Maude's father, John R. McFie, was president of the original Board of Regents for the newly created New Mexico A&M College. Lansing B. Bloom, Maude's husband, edited her thesis with the aim of publishing it. Jo Tice Bloom, Maude's daughter-in-law, undertook to continue the project of documenting this piece of New Mexico history. Her introduction portrays a fascinating and accomplished woman. (1880–1973). Amazon Book Reviews.

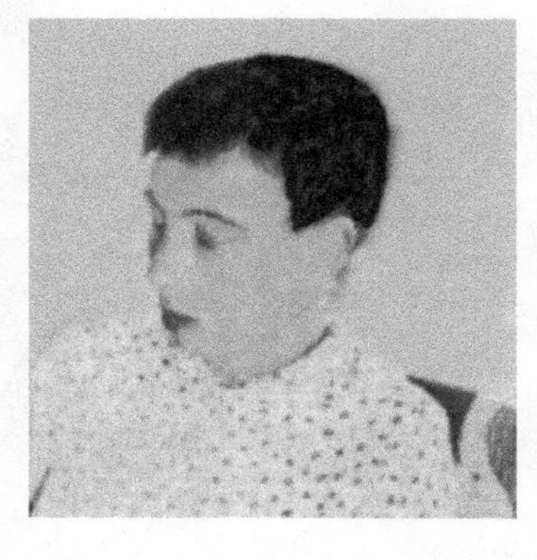

E. Boyd. Courtesy of Sunstone Press.

Boyd, E., PhD. Santos authority. (Ms. Boyd preferred the gender-neutral usage of E. Boyd over her birth name of Elizabeth Boyd White). Boyd's book, *Saints and Saintmakers of New Mexico,* established her as an authority on the subject. It is considered the first truly scholarly and well-researched book on santos (painted or carved wooden images of saints common to the southwestern United States). An acknowledged scholar, researcher, and curator emeritus of Spanish colonial arts for the Museum of New Mexico, Boyd also studied embroidery, interior design, and painting at the Pennsylvania Academy of the Fine Arts before attending the Académie de la Grande Chaumière in Paris. She moved to Santa Fe in 1929 and began exhibiting her paintings. In 1933, she co-founded and began exhibiting with the Rio Grande Painters. After the group disbanded in 1936, Boyd received funding from the US General Services Administration to paint watercolors and to conduct research documenting designs from eighteenth and nineteenth century artifacts in New Mexico. Boyd was a prolific writer, contributing to numerous historical journals and popular publications. The culmination of her life's research was the publication in 1968 of *Popular Arts of Colonial New Mexico*, which was twelve years in the making. (1903–1974). *Notable New Mexico Women.*

Ella Louise McGruder Boyer.

Boyer, Ella Louise McGruder. Co-founder of Blackdom. Ella Louise McGruder Boyer and her husband, Francis (Frank) Marion Boyer, co-founded the African American community of Blackdom in Chaves County, New Mexico, with approximately one dozen other African American families in 1901. Among them were Ella's sister and her husband, Dan Keyes. A graduate of the Haines Institute in Augusta, Georgia, Ella followed her quest for opportunity to New Mexico. Founded under the requirements of the Homestead Act, Blackdom experienced significant growth in the first decades of the twentieth century with African American settlers from throughout the United States moving there. Blackdom represented an opportunity to those who wanted to shape their own destiny at a time when choices for African Americans were extremely limited. The community remained viable until its abandonment in the mid-1920s for lack of good water and because of restrictions on drilling new wells. Francis Boyer was a graduate of the historic Black Morehouse College in Atlanta, then a homesteader and farmer and Ella was a school teacher. The Boyers left Blackdom for Vado in the Mesilla Valley near Las Cruces to begin another all-black community. (1873–1965). New Mexico Historic Scenic Markers. From the Office of the State Historian. New Mexico, September 16, 2016.

Rebecca A. Brewer.
Courtesy of Mimbres Region Arts Council Youth Mural Program.

Brewer, Rebecca A. Madame Brewer, La Negra, Rebecca. A reputed healer and namesake of Brewer Hill in Silver City, Rebecca Brewer was born in Macon, Georgia, the daughter of freed slaves. Around age thirty-two she traveled alone to Silver City at the urging of her family to seek a better climate for her tuberculosis. There she attained both health and wealth. The late Silver City historian Luis Perez called her "a mysterious yet prominent woman...cast in the bronze of history in the same manner as other strong Silver City females..." She was a large, striking Black woman and a practitioner of natural healing, a curandera. Local children called her "La Negra". She told fortunes, made potions, and cast spells. She initially made a living as a masseuse. Brewer said she had learned from her parents how to diagnose illness and which herbs could heal. She was once charged with practicing medicine without a license and was arrested but paid the $1,000 cash bond, and the charges were dropped. She arrived in Silver City as a Roman Catholic, but might have been excommunicated because of assisting with pregnancy terminations. She also was known for providing certain essential medical services for the denizens of a brothel on the hill just below her home. The area where she amassed considerable real estate, once called Sonora Hill, came to be known as Brewer Hill. She lived there as well, donating land and a building for the Brewer Hill Baptist Church. It was attended by the Black people of the area, since they were not welcome in other congregations. Perez wrote that Brewer was remembered as "a charitable woman who did much to help poor people..." A note in *Noteworthy Black Women of New Mexico* has her last name as "Briever." (1868–1969). *Desert Exposure. Noteworthy Black Women of New Mexico. Silver City Daily Press and Independent*, February 22, 2006. Essay by Luis Perez.

Brewster, Mela Sedillo. Folk dance specialist and activist. Mela Brewster came from an established New Mexico colonial Hispanic family involved in politics and local affairs. Mela adhered to this pathway, even though she taught fine arts and drama at the University of New Mexico, painted, and lectured on Spanish colonial arts. That led to teaching Mexican and New Mexican folk dance. She was one of two Hispanic instructors at the University of New Mexico in 1933 involved in protesting prejudice by Anglo-Americans in fraternities and sororities against Hispanic students. In the 1940s she contributed stories for the Federal Writers Project and worked on *New Mexico-A Guide to the Colorful State*, published by the Works Progress Administration (WPA). She organized festivals for the Federal Music Program and helped with the WPA song books. She also published work on Spanish and Mexican folk dances and arts. In 1942 Mela and her husband, Robert Koeber, bought the Refugio Gomez House (1875), a registered historic property in Albuquerque and preserved its traditional New Mexico Territorial features. Later, the couple was active in grassroots Democratic politics. (1907–1989). *Women in Education: New Mexico. Biographies of New Mexico Women.*

Maralyn Budke. *Santa Fe New Mexican.*

Budke, Maralyn. Knew her numbers. Maralyn Budke was a 1967 political science graduate of the University of New Mexico. Ten years later, she became chief of staff for Governor David Cargo. From there, she moved to the important state Legislative Finance Committee (LFC) and later became its first woman director, a post she held for fourteen years. A protégée of Inez Gill, Budke was "a brilliant strategist and trusted advisor [to two governors]." Among the original staff of the LFC when it was founded in 1951, Budke served as fiscal analyst on its finance committee. Budke and Gill have been called two of the "most important and influential women in New Mexico state government." Garrey Carruthers, the other governor Budke served, said of her, "She stands with the finest of governors, senators, congressmen and all other public servants in terms of contributions to our state." Supported by family wealth, Budke retired from state service at age forty-six to devote herself to charitable pursuits. (1936–2010). *Santa Fe Living Treasures—Elder Stories.* New Mexico Historic Women Marker Initiative.

Bullock, Alice. Historian, author. Alice Bullock was born into her avocation with an insatiable love of learning. "I can't remember when I couldn't read," she once said although residents of the coal camps she grew up in Oklahoma and New Mexico could scarcely afford reading matter. Once her mother purchased a complete set of the works of Charles Dickens from a traveling book salesman but was dismayed to learn her daughter had read them all before the final payment was due. After beginning work at age eleven at a coal company hospital and later as a maid, she attended New Mexico Normal School in Las Vegas (later New Mexico Highlands University), earning a teaching certificate. Later she taught in tiny ranching and mining communities in northern New Mexico which formed the basis of her later writing. She met her husband Dale Bullock when he interviewed her for his newspaper the *Raton Reporter*. Her writing career began after the couple moved to Santa Fe and she wrote a history of the Santa Fe schools. In the 1950s she wrote hundreds of fictional pieces under the pen name Bill Bullock, because she felt editors of Western magazines would be hesitant to accept articles from a woman. To aid her work, Bullock visited the small towns of the state collecting folklore, history, and photographs to accompany her articles. She is the author of *Living Legends of the Santa Fe Country, Mountain Villages, Loretto and the Miraculous Staircase*, and *Monumental Ghosts*, all from Sunstone Press. In her later years, Bullock reviewed books for several New Mexico journals. (1904–1986). *Santa Fe New Mexican.*

Ruth Leah Bernheim Bunzel.
Courtesy of Jewish Women's Archives.

Bunzel, Ruth Leah Bernheim. Student of Zuni mythology and pottery. Ruth Bunzel was another protégé of Franz Boas, who believed fieldwork required "both men and women to really get a whole picture of culture." Bunzel began her career as Boas's secretary and ended as an accomplished anthropologist. She broke new ground on the art and creative process of the Zuni people. She saw anthropology as a means to understand not only others but also ourselves. In 1924, she accompanied anthropologist Ruth Benedict to western New Mexico and east-central Arizona to study the Zuni and followed Boas's suggestion to put her typewriter aside for her own research on a topic that interested her, the artist's relationship to work. Bunzel felt that "society consisted of more than old men with long memories." She was drawn to the Zuni because women were the potters and wielded considerable societal power. Bunzel subsequently began graduate study in anthropology at Columbia University. In 1929, she received her PhD with publication of a landmark book, *The Pueblo Potter*. Rather than focusing on the objects of art, Bunzel was the first anthropologist to analyze artists' feelings, their relationship to their work, and the process of creativity. To understand how artists work within the confines of traditional styles,

Bunzel apprenticed herself to Zuni potters and became a respected, skilled potter. A prolific scholar, she also contributed an understanding of Zuni cosmology closely by producing important work on Zuni values, language, culture, and personality. Bunzel's work provided much of the material for Benedict's synthesis of Zuni in *Patterns of Culture.* In addition to the Zuni, Bunzel wrote about other native peoples of the southwestern United States. Her detailed fieldwork and writings are known for their great sensitivity (1898–1990). *Daughters of the Desert.* Jewish Women's Archives.

Butler, Lettia Parsons. Gained fame as a nurse. Lettia Parsons Butler distinguished herself in many ways, according to *Bridges: New Mexico Black Women, 1900–1950.* Perhaps one of her bravest acts, even more so than serving as a nurse in her hometown of Santa Fe during epidemics despite her lack of formal training, was her desire to maintain her racial identity. Butler was of mixed French, Indian, and Black ancestry of Louisiana parentage, and *Bridges: New Mexico Black Women, 1900-1950* observes that it would have been easy for her to pass as white. Contemporary photos depict her as a striking woman of regular white features. Butler's insistence on identifying with her race went so far as to send her daughters to the all-Black Fisk University in Nashville, Tennessee, for their college education. A staunch Catholic, she married a former US Army bugler at Fort Union. The Butlers ran a hotel and supported their church financially and through acts of piety. *Bridges: New Mexico Black Women, 1900–1950* called her a "ball of dynamite" with a "take charge attitude and commanding voice." (1866–1951). *Bridges: New Mexico Black Women. 1900–1950.*

Carty, Susan, Mother Praxedes. "Serving God by serving others." Mother Praxedes was born Susan Carty in Ireland in 1854, one of 11 children. As a girl, she acted as a guide to a blind beggar woman after she heard her priest say that to serve God was to serve others. By 1874, the aspiring nun had moved to the United States where she took her vows as a novice with the Sisters of Loretto in Kentucky. She was given the name Sister Praxedes. Soon after, she contracted tuberculosis and was sent to Santa Fe, where it was hoped the climate would help. Her health improved, and she became fluent in Spanish and took her final vows. In 1878 Sister Praxedes was given responsibility for a school in Bernalillo, educating young girls and planting gardens for self-sufficiency. After improving the school, she began fundraising to restore St. Genevieve's Church, which was rebuilt in 1886. When Mother Praxedes left Las Cruces, she was hailed as one of the most beloved leaders the community had ever known. Her commitment to education, hard work, and self-sufficiency, along with her business sense, made her a natural "trouble-shooter" and the ideal candidate to run schools. Mother Praxedes was appointed to head Loretto schools in Missouri and Colorado, and in 1896 she was called to Kentucky as Superior General, a position she held twenty-six years. She worked tirelessly, travelling to Rome three times to meet with the Pope, dispatching nuns to nurse the sick during an influenza epidemic, and overseeing the establishment of fifty-one Loretto academies. In 1916, Mother Praxedes oversaw the construction of the first women's Catholic College in the American West, Loretto College in Missouri, and planned the first foreign mission of the Loretto Order to China. After retiring in 1922, Mother Praxedes moved to El Paso to help build Loretto Academy, acclaimed as "...one of the finest souls to see the necessity of higher education for women." (1854–1933). https://www.irelandsown.ie/mother-praxedes-carty-serving-god-by-serving-others. *Women in Education: New Mexico*.

Ina Cassidy.

Cassidy, Barnum Sizer Perlina, "Ina." Writer, sculptor, suffragist, teacher, lecturer, promoter of the arts. Ina Barnum was born on a Colorado cattle ranch but moved East to attend Columbia University. There she became involved in the suffrage movement. She worked hard for the movement on the local level before turning to the national scene. She met artist Gerald Cassidy, and the two were married in 1912. The Cassidys moved to Santa Fe soon after and became part of its growing artists and writers' establishment. As a writer, Cassidy turned out a number of interesting titles. Who would not want to read her *American Natural Food and Edible Weeds*? From 1931 to 1960, she wrote a monthly column for the *New Mexico Magazine* promoting the state as an arts scene. As an artist, Ina exhibited her sculptures at the Museum of New Mexico and at the New Mexico State Fair. As an arts promoter, she served as the New Mexico Director of the Federal Writers Project from 1935 to 1939, assisting with the effort to combat the state's high illiteracy rate. She was active in a number of civic and cultural organizations, including the American Indian Defense Association, the New Mexico Association on Indian Affairs, the Spanish Colonial Arts Society, the Historical Society of New Mexico, and the National League of American Pen Women. She also was a charter member of the National League of Women Voters in New Mexico. (1869–1965). *Artists of the Canyons and Caminos: Santa Fe, the Early Years. Notable New Mexico Women. Famous and Unusual Gravesites in New Mexico History.*

Cata, Regina Albarado. Led the revival. Regina Cata was born in Colorado where her father had moved from Spain. She married a native of San Juan Pueblo and spent her life assisting its people preserve and renew their arts and customs. Cata was one of a handful of New Mexico pueblo potters leading the 1930s "San Juan Revival." She and her husband Demicio, to whom she would be married for sixty-three years, also were making revival style, polychrome redware by the end of the decade. Her crafts club visited the Museum of New Mexico to examine authentic San Juan pottery. Cata and her fellow San Juan potters also visited an archaeological site, Potsuwi'i. Here they found incised pottery made by the the Pueblo's ancestors. She also wove a tapestry of the Virgin of Guadalupe which hangs in her village church. The tapestry was dedicated to World War II service members from the Pueblo. Regina Cata made thousands of cloth dolls and clay sculptures. Her work is displayed in the Smithsonian Institution. She was still active at the age of 90. (ca. 1881–unknown). *Indian Pottery: 750 Artist Biographies. Women in Education: New Mexico.*

Willa Sibert Cather.

Cather, Willa Sibert, "Willie." Chronicler of the Southwest. Willa Cather called New Mexico the "most beautiful country I have ever seen anywhere," adding that she was "almost sure [I] could work here." She did, writing portions of *Death Comes for the Archbishop* in Mary Austin's Santa Fe home. Later, when Austin criticized the book, Cather denied that any part of it had been written there. But the inscription for Cather's presentation copy to her, reads, "For Mary Austin, in whose lovely study I wrote the last chapter of this book." In *The Selected Letters of Willa Cather*, Edith Lewis wrote that Cather located a copy of *The Life of the Right Reverend Joseph H. Machebeuf* and "There, in a single evening, as...the idea of *Death Comes for the Archbishop* came to her, essentially as she afterwards wrote it." Lawrence Clark Powell said *Death Comes for the Archbishop* "justly ranks in the highest realm of American literature." Cather often called it her best work, acknowledging she never expected to write about the Southwest because "it was too big and too various." Cather explained that, although she had known the Southwest "early, and knew it long and well," she did not write about it earlier, because "the Southwest is so essentially and at its roots a Catholic country" and that "no Protestant could handle material [about it] properly." When after fifteen years no Catholic writer stepped forward, Cather did. (1873–1947). *Southwest Classics. The Selected Letters of Willa Cather.*

Faro and Doris Caudill. Farm Security Administration.

Caudill, Doris. Pie Town Woman and homesteader. Doris Caudill was one of a handful of determined women who, along with their husbands and families, homesteaded in Pie Town, New Mexico, at the height of the Great Depression until just before World War II. This they did on inadequate and insufficient land provided by the US Government. Their efforts could be seen as a public relations stunt to prove that Americans could still make it by the sweat of their brows at a time when the country's economic picture seemed so bleak that some feared the country was teetering on the edge of revolution. As Joan Myers relates in *Pie Town Woman*, Caudill's was the "tale of a patented dream of moving west...a woman's way of making good on her dreams." Instead, the next ten years proved a daily struggle for survival. Caudill and her family and other Texans and Okies who had been "dusted out" and who thought they could find a better life on the arid plains of western New Mexico grubbed out rock-hard land to raise pinto beans and anything else they could eat, barter, or sell. For them, the term "dirt poor" took on real meaning as they eked out a living and slept on a dirt floor in a half-dugout shelter. As Caudill's husband wryly put it when they finally left for much better economic wartime defense jobs in Albuquerque, "Farewell old homestead. I bid you adieu. I may go to hell, but I'll never come back to you." (birth and death dates not found). *Pie Town Woman.*

Dorothy Cave.

Cave, Dorothy (pen name) aka Mrs. Jack Aldrich, nickname Dolly. Dorothy Cave spent much of her childhood exploring with her geologist father the isolated villages and mountains of northern New Mexico. Although her formal education was at Agnes Scott College and the Universities of Colorado and Wyoming, she believed her true education came from these remote but vanishing hamlets and pueblos and from the soil-rooted wisdom of those who lived in them. Dolly traveled widely, danced with the Atlanta Ballet while at Agnes Scott, acted, and taught. She is the author of two histories: *Beyond Courage*, which won the New Mexico Presswomen's Zia Award, and *Four Trails to Valor*, both from Sunstone Press. Her two novels, *Mountains of the Blue Stone* and *Song on a Blue Guitar* were also published by Sunstone Press, in addition to *God's Warrior, Father Albert Braun, OFM, Last of the Frontier Priests*. Cave served as historical consultant for two documentary films: *Colors of Courage*, produced by Scott Henry and E. Anthony Martinez for the University of New Mexico's Center for Regional Studies; and for Aaron Wilson's award-winning *A New Mexico Story*, based largely on *Beyond Courage*. She appeared in both as narrator/commentator. *Beyond Courage* focused on the members of the New Mexico National Guard who were kept captive after the notorious Bataan Death March. The book inspired composer Steven Melillo's acclaimed musical opus of the same title. Dolly and her husband Jack travelled around the world doing research and interviews for that book and her many subsequent books. In 2018 she was presented a Congressional Award from Congressman Steve Pearce. (1927–2020). James Clois Smith, Jr., Sunstone Press. https://www.tributearchive.com/obituaries/19082460/Dorothy-Cave-Aldrich. Find A Grave Memorial.

Chabot, Mary Lea (Maria). Advocate and friend of Georgia O'Keeffe. Maria Chabot was an advocate for New Mexico artists and writers during Works Progress Administration (WPA) days and later for Native American arts. She was a friend of famed artist Georgia O'Keeffe, serving as general contractor for O'Keeffe's house in Abiquiú, often referring to herself as the "hired man." Chabot took the famous photograph of O'Keeffe entitled the "Woman Who Rode Away," in which the artist is shown perched on the back of a motorcycle. The correspondence between the two was published in *Maria Chabot—Georgia O'Keeffe: Correspondence 1941–1949.* Editors Barbara Buhler Lynes and Ann Paden note that the two were drawn to each other for different reasons. "O'Keeffe needed capable help to sustain and provision her remote household, and although Chabot [half O'Keeffe's age] needed a place to live where she could pursue her writing with minimum distraction, she was also seeking a mentor." Chabot also edited a series of articles on Indian arts and crafts for *New Mexico Magazine.* (1913–2001). *Maria Chabot—Georgia O'Keeffe: Correspondence 1941–1949.*

Marjorie Bell Chambers.
The battle for civil rights, or, how Los Alamos became a county. F802.L84 C47 1999.

Chambers, Marjorie Bell, PhD. Historian, educator, activist, presidential advisor. Marjorie Bell Chambers advised governors and presidents, participated in the formation of the United Nations, and headed two women's colleges. She married and subsequently raised four children while pursuing her education, culminating in a doctorate from the University of New Mexico. Marjorie was a passionate women's rights activist, educator, and politician. She was the first woman in New Mexico to run for Congress and for lieutenant governor. She was an advisor to several presidents of the United States and governors of New Mexico. She was a dean and graduate school professor of the Union Institute and University in Cincinnati, Ohio, for twenty-five years. Marjorie was also the president of Colorado Women's College. As a dedicated women's rights activist for more than fifty years, she left an impressive legacy. A spokesperson and national leader of the cause for passage of the Equal Rights Amendment (ERA), she became a leader for the adoption of the measure in New Mexico. She also worked tirelessly with the Girl Scouts of America for sixty-nine years. (1923–2006). *Albuquerque Journal*, August 25, 2006. New Mexico Historic Women Marker Initiative.

Chapman, Kate Antonia Muller. Adobe was her legacy. Kate Chapman championed traditional New Mexico builders and their methods. As Catherine Colby writes in her biography of Chapman, being a mother, poet, adventurer, and social activist might not have been that unusual in 1930s Santa Fe, but "to venture in the predominantly male field of adobe construction sets her apart." Colby observes that in the early century, many well-educated women with a rebellious spirit, artists and writers among them, were attracted to northern New Mexico. But what Chapman accomplished was "rare for a woman." One example among many: Margetta Dietrich bought three properties on Santa Fe's Canyon Road to save them from redevelopment then restored them under Chapman's direction. With friend Dorothy N. Stewart, Chapman co-authored *Adobe Notes or How to Keep the Weather Out with Just Plain Mud*. Colby sums up Chapman's life thusly: "Kate Chapman relished life and challenged current mores." (1887–1944). *Kate Chapman: Adobe Builder in 1930s Santa Fe*.

Denise Chavez.

Chavez, Denise. Teller of tales. With a diverse career in literature, Denise Chavez's honors include the American Book Award, the New Mexico Governor's Award in Literature, the Premio Aztlán Literary Prize, and the Hispanic Heritage Award for Literature. Among her more than a dozen novels, plays, and works of nonfiction are *What It Is—What It Was!*, *Face of an Angel*, *The Last of the Menu Girls*, *Loving Pedro Infante*, *Shattering the Myth: Plays by Hispanic*

Women, and *The King and Queen of Comezón. A Taco Testimony: Meditations on Family, Food and Culture* is part paean to the taco, some of which reads, "We offer up this meal with gratitude. We remember that tacos are one of life's greatest blessings. We remember that tacos are sacred." She calls the book "[M]y story of nourishment, of culture, and how I came to know who I am..." Perhaps food also played a role in her family's views on racial identity, especially as it pertained to Chicano or Hispanic identification. "My father would never admit to being a Mexican married to a Mexican," Chavez observed. "The distinction between Spanish and Mexican is a sore point in our broken, unspoken-about New Mexico [family] that few care to think about, with its racism and divisions between Spanish and Mexican. Northern New Mexicans consider themselves Spanish, while many of us who live in the south consider ourselves Mexican." She recalls, "I come from a poor people who didn't acknowledge that they were poor." (1948–). *A Taco Testimony: Meditations on Family, Food and Culture.*

Soledad Chavez de Chacón. *Albuquerque Journal.*

Chavez de Chacón, Soledad. New Mexico's first woman governor. Soledad Chavez de Chacón presided over New Mexico government for two weeks in the summer of 1924, thus becoming the first woman to serve as the state's chief executive. Chacón, a Democrat, had been elected Secretary of State in 1922, just two years after women earned the right to vote and a year after the New Mexico Constitution was amended to allow them to seek office. She was the first woman elected Secretary of State and one of the first two women elected to statewide office in New Mexico. And she was the first Hispanic woman in the country to win statewide elective office. Chacón believed that, "By the ballot, women would be able to bring about many things for the benefit of women and children that men have refused or neglected to make possible." Born into a prominent, middle-class family, she was active in literary, artistic, and issues-oriented clubs and supported women's suffrage. But a political career likely was not on her mind when some influential Democrats knocked on her kitchen door in 1922 and asked her to hurry over to the party's state convention. "My mother did not solicit the nomination," Adelina Chacón Ward recalls. "She was in the kitchen baking a cake, and I saw the car pull up outside." Chavez agreed to the nomination after consulting with both her husband and father. Democrats swept the election, and Chavez started her two-year term. In May 1924, Lieutenant Governor Jose A. Baca died unexpectedly. When Governor James F. Hinkle headed to New York the next month for the Democratic National Convention, Chavez was next in line. Chavez believed her 1924 elevation was the first time in the United States a woman had been called on to assume such responsibilities. It was her "earnest desire to carry out the plans and wishes of our governor during his absence, in as fearless and conscientious a manner as has been his policy," she said. Her service ended when Hinkle returned to Santa Fe on July 5, 1924. Chavez was reelected to a two-year term as Secretary of State in 1924. Historian Charles F. Coan notes Chacón possessed an unusual fitness for public office, being painstaking and careful, prompt and courteous and inspired. Chavez was in her second year as a member of the House of Representatives when she died in August 1936 of peritonitis. She would have turned 46 years old a week later. (1890–1936). *Albuquerque Journal*, Deborah Baker, October 24, 2010. *Notable New Mexico Women. New Mexico Women Legislators Since Statehood.*

Judy Chicago. *Albuquerque Journal.*

Chicago, Judy. Artist, feminist. Born Judy Cohen in Chicago, the artist changed her name to the place of her birth to "assert her independence." She has lived in New Mexico for more than 30 years. The *Albuquerque Journal* says her work explores mythological representations of women and creation. The newspaper said her work "defiantly resists patriarchy with a searing intensity." One collection is called "The Birth Project from New Mexico Collections." Chicago uses birth as a metaphor for creation. Chicago's work incorporates a variety of artistic skills, such as needlework, counterbalanced with labor-intensive skills such as welding and pyrotechnics. (1939–). *Albuquerque Journal.* Kathaleen Roberts. May 26, 2019.

Sallie Robert Chisum.

Chisum, Sallie Robert. First Lady of Artesia. Sallie Chisum was nineteen years old when she arrived from Texas at her Uncle John Chisum's Jinglebob Land and Livestock Company Ranch south of Roswell. Her ranching skills rivaled those of the cowboys she joined, driving cattle up her uncle's Goodnight-Loving Trail to Colorado. She and her second husband opened the first post office and reading room in what became Artesia, New Mexico. Her landholdings are part of Artesia's original townsite and include the site of her cast stone home. Her diaries include entries about her uncle, Billy the Kid, the Regulators, and the Lincoln County War. (1858–1936). New Mexico Historic Marker Initiative.

Peggy Pond Church.

Church, Peggy Pond. Forever linked to Otowi Bridge. In *The House at Otowi Bridge*, Peggy Pond Church offers an intimate, lyrical portrait of her friend Edith Warren. Oliver LaFarge called *The House at Otowi Bridge* "a finely told tale of a strange land and of a rare character who united with it and, without seeming to do anything to that end, exerted an unusual influence upon all lovers of that soil with whom she came in contact." Church's association with northern New Mexico can be traced to her girlhood. A poet and children's author, Church was known as "The First Lady of New Mexico Poetry." (1903–1986). *The House at Otowi Bridge*. New Mexico Historic Women Marker Initiative. *Buried Treasures: Famous and Unusual Gravesites in New Mexico History*.

Ann Nolan Clark.

Clark, Ann Nolan (pseudonym Marie Dunn). Noted children's author. *Women in Education: New Mexico* called Ann Nolan Clark "a pioneer" in writing about and for Indian children. In 1953, she won the Newbery Medal for the most distinguished American children's book, *Secret of the Andes*. Her books include *In My Mother's House*, *Medicine Man's Daughter*, and *Along Sandy Trails*. Clark taught English at Highlands University in Las Vegas, New Mexico, but, in the early 1920s, transitioned into teaching reading to Native American children at Tesuque Pueblo. In so doing she involved the entire village so that parents acquired an understanding and a favorable view of education. During that 25-year tenure, Clark found the underfunded Tesuque School could not afford any substantial instructional material, so she produced it. In the process of teaching the children about literature, she incorporated their voices and stories to write *In My Mother's House* and other children's books. She described this process in her adult nonfiction book, *Journey to the People*. The Bureau of Indian Affairs published 15 of Clark's books, all relating to her experiences with Native Americans. *In My Mother's House*, illustrated by Pueblo artist Velino Herrera, was named a Caldecott Honor book in 1942. (1898–1995*). Notable New Mexico Women. Women in Education: New Mexico.*

.Agnes Morley Cleaveland.

Cleaveland, Agnes Morley. Exemplar of fortitude, Agnes Morley Cleaveland modeled fortitude in *No Life for a Lady*, her noted chronicle of growing into womanhood in western New Mexico's Datil Mountains in the years immediately preceding statehood. For Cleaveland, the burning question, in cowboy parlance, centered on was she "good enough to take along?" Her tales of riding herd on the open range, branding cattle, fighting droughts and blizzards, and hunting marked her as "a born storyteller," balancing "realism and humor" as she unfolded her stories of growing up on the ranch with her beloved brother Ray. Because of her ranching heritage, Cleaveland harbored an enmity for the homesteaders who flocked to free government land near Pie Town. She encouraged Conrad Richter to write of it in his cattle industry-biased novel *The Sea of Grass.* Cleaveland again attempted to write something equal to her first book. She finally published *Satan's Paradise*, stories emanating from her birthplace of Cimarron, New Mexico. A more personal, private side is revealed in *Open Range: The Life of Agnes Morley Cleaveland* by Darlis A. Miller. It is the painful story of a failed teenaged marriage, the lifelong care of a disabled daughter, adherence to and banishment from the Christian Scientist faith, fervent stewardship of woman's suffrage, a lifetime friendship with Lou Henry (Mrs. Herbert) Hoover, a seismic political shift from socialism to conservatism, and ultimately near blindness. She had lived away from New Mexico for years, finally returning at age 72 to live the next 11 years of her life. (1874–1958). *No Life for a Lady. The Sea of Grass. Open Range: The Life of Agnes Morley Cleaveland. Satan's Paradise. Notable New Mexico Women.*

Cline, Dorothy I., PhD. Politician, educator. A lifelong Democrat, Dorothy Cline was active in the League of Women Voters in Ohio, where she worked to repeal the 18th Amendment (Prohibition) before moving to Albuquerque. There she took up liberal causes and taught at the University of New Mexico. She was recognized for her expertise in state and urban government and politics and taught in that field for many years. Cline was acknowledged for helping gain awareness and funding in public education. She was cited for her "strong influence" on working for the betterment of New Mexico public service in the classroom, as well as by setting an example in elective and appointive office. Upon her death, the *Albuquerque Journal* editorialized, "Hers were important, significant contributions to New Mexico." (1905–1993). *Albuquerque Journal. Notable New Mexico Women. Women in Education: New Mexico.*

Clingenpeel, Frances M. Brought educational TV into New Mexico living rooms. In 1965 Frances Clingenpeel worked with KNME-TV in Albuquerque to prepare and present a series of programs for parents of children entering first grade. The program was called "Preparing the Child for School" and was the first attempt in New Mexico to prepare youngsters for school through the mass media. Clingenpeel worked for Albuquerque Public Schools, a co-sponsor with the University of New Mexico of KNME, for 40 years. She was a member of various professional organizations involved with education. (ca. 1911–1994). *Women in Education: New Mexico.*

Cockerell, Wilmatte Porter. Teacher, naturalist, author, lecturer. Wilmatte Cockerell was distinguished for the numerous species of fauna and flora she discovered and collected. Many are named for her. She was among the first science faculty members of the New Mexico Normal School (now Highlands University) in Las Vegas where she met her future husband. An Englishman, Theodore Cockerell came to America with his children after his first wife's death. Following her marriage, Wilmatte immediately began collecting specimens with her famous husband. They travelled the world in pursuit of science. Between them, they contributed to the fields of botany, entomology, taxonomy, paleontology, evolution, and plant conservation. Wilmatte never lost her passion for teaching. She taught high school, and after Theodore retired the two worked as volunteers to educate children about science and conservation. In addition to teaching, Wilmatte went on expeditions, both alone and with Theodore. She wrote scientific papers on her botanical findings. The website Smart Bitches, Trashy Books notes "She also made an income from selling specimens. One of her discoveries was a red sunflower that she found not in some far-flung location but across the street from her house. It was a mutant variety that she was able to transplant to her own garden, cultivate, and sell to seed companies." (1869–1957). *Women in Education: New Mexico.* https://smartbitchestrashybooks.com/tag/wilmatte-porter-cockerell/.

Coe, Louise Holland. Shattered New Mexico Senate's glass ceiling. Louise Coe was a former teacher and superintendent of schools in Lincoln County where she and her husband ranched. Coe was a strong advocate for higher education and the first woman in the New Mexico State Senate. Of that role, Coe believed she needed the courtesy of her fellow lawmakers, "but I most certainly didn't need any help in making up my mind how to vote." She was the youngest person to serve, being elected to four consecutive terms. As chairman of the Senate Education Committee for ten years, she was influential in securing legislation to upgrade schools, obtain free textbooks, get larger libraries, and secure higher teacher qualifications and salaries. She also oversaw school consolidation. After leaving state government, she made an unsuccessful bid for Congress. Coe believed that women should participate fully in the political life of their state and country. "Everybody should take it for granted that the female half of the species plays a strong political role along with every other role in society." (1894–1985). *Notable New Mexico Women. Women in Education: New Mexico.* Find A Memorial. *Santa Fe New Mexican*, December 9, 1984. *New Mexico Women Legislators Since Statehood.*

Anita Scott Coleman.

Coleman, Anita Scott. Harlem Renaissance figure. Although Anita Scott Coleman achieved national prominence after leaving New Mexico, it was in Silver City where she attained her education and began her distinguished writing career. Scott, the daughter of a former Buffalo Soldier, was born in Guaymas, Mexico. She was raised on her father's one hundred-sixty-acre homestead south of Silver City and was its Normal School's first African-American graduate in 1909. After several years of teaching, she married James Harold Coleman. They lived on the family farm before moving to Los Angeles in 1926. Scott's first short stories, published while she lived in New Mexico, marked the beginning of a thirty-year writing career. She published stories, poems, and essays in several national magazines and two books, as well as writing for the movies. Today, she is considered an important literary figure often linked with such Harlem Renaissance giants as Langston Hughes. As the late Felipe de Ortego y Gasca put it, "In the desert air of the Hispanic Southwest, Anita Scott Coleman did not bloom unseen nor [were] her words] wasted in the desert air." Calling Scott "a prodigious writer, widely read in her time," de Ortego y Gasca added that "[t]hough duly recognized in her day the foliage of time has o'er bloomed her name and works." Coleman has been the subject of two books and a half dozen scholarly essays. Biographers Cynthia Davis and Verner D. Mitchel observe that, because Scott left no journals and only a handful of letters, scholars must look to her stories, some semi-autobiographical, to form a picture of her life. (1890–1960). *Western Echoes of the Harlem Renaissance: The Life and Writings of Anita Scott Coleman. Afro-Hispanic Writer Anita Scott and the Harlem Renaissance West. The Independent: The Silver City Daily Press*, November 5, 2015.

Mary Elizabeth Jane Colter.

Colter, Mary Elizabeth Jane. Fred Harvey architect, designer. Innovation, flair, and imagination coupled with fidelity to Southwestern culture underscored Mary Colter's career as Fred Harvey's chief architect and designer for more than forty years. She was among the first to appreciate the importance of Indian and Spanish design and architecture encountered throughout the territory encompassed by the Harvey hotels and restaurants. Following Colter's temporary stints designing the Indian Building at the Alvarado Hotel in Albuquerque in 1902, followed by design of the Hopi House at the Grand Canyon three years later, Harvey executives wanted a full-time employee. They needed a full-time employee to maintain the chain's standards of quality and good taste—someone with a background in architecture, a person familiar with Spanish and Indian culture, an individual, writes Virginia L. Grattan in *Mary Colter: Builder Upon the Red Earth*, "with style and imagination" possessing the "force of personality" to see ideas through to construction. In Mary Elizabeth Jane Colter they found exactly that individual. As a graduate of the California School of Design augmented by an architectural apprenticeship with Harvey, this formidable woman fit their bill exactly. Writes Grattan, "Colter was a perfectionist. She could be dogmatic and intractable. She knew the effect she wanted and pursued it relentlessly." She was demanding of everyone, herself foremost. Colter always pictured in her mind the effect she wanted and allowed nothing to get in the way of bringing it to fruition." In all this, Colter was guided by her philosophy of what a building was. Grattan says Colter's idea was that "a building should grow out of its setting, embodying its history and flavor of location. It should belong to its environment as though indigenous to that spot." This she achieved through such magnificent structures as the Watchtower and Bright Angel Lodge at the Grand Canyon and La Posada in Winslow, Arizona, to name a few. Examples of her decorating genius can still be found at Santa Fe's landmark lodging destination, the La Fonda Hotel, where her influence was once to be found in every room. Colter returned to Santa Fe to live out the ten last years of her retirement, dying there in 1958. A few years before her death, Colter declared, "There's no such thing as living too long." (1869–1958). *Mary Colter: Builder Upon the Red Earth*. New Mexico Historic Women Marker Initiative. *Buried Treasures: Famous and Unusual Gravesites in New Mexico History*.

Helen Quintana Cordero.

Cordero, Helen Quintana. "Storyteller" potter. The story and art of Cochiti potter Helen Quintana Cordero are shared in *The Pueblo Storyteller* by Barbara A. Babcock and Guy and Doris Monthan. Calling her "a master potter," they write, "Her vision was an inspired one: drawing upon venerable traditions of the past, aware of the unspoken ...rules which guide those traditions, she chose to innovate." Cordero said her storytellers depicted her grandfather and that "[h]is eyes are closed because he is thinking and his mouth is open because he's telling stories." She added that, "All my potteries come out of my heart. They're my little people. I talk to them and they're singing. If you're listening, you can hear them." (1915– 1994). *The Pueblo Storyteller*.

Cox, "Grandma" Josephine Anderson. The Angel of the Pecos. During the flu epidemic of 1918, Grandma Josephine Cox fearlessly led other women in nursing and feeding the sick in tents and shacks along the banks of the Pecos River in Carlsbad, New Mexico. The little white-haired angel worked day and night. All sixty patients in her care regained their health, leading to her nickname, "The Angel of the Pecos." Although the epidemic passed, she continued her work ministering to the needs of the sick in her community. Although Grandma had no formal medical training, she was a natural in her field, and her impressive healing gifts helped many. With her husband's support, she opened a sanatorium for tuberculosis victims. Carlsbad's dry climate was ideal for people suffering with the disease, and many people from the East came there, hoping to regain their health. Grandma was known for her pleasant disposition, loving nature, and exceptional healing ability. The "Angel of the Pecos" lived a long life dedicated to helping others. She was also a lifelong artist who stopped painting only when she lost her eyesight late in life. Grandma died at age 92. (1849–1941). New Mexico Women Historic Marker Initiative.

Amber Kanazbah Crotty.

Crotty, Amber Kanazbah. Spotlights sexual assaults on Native American women. Amber Crotty works with advocates and her Navajo community members to increase awareness of missing and murdered Navajo people through public advocacy. Crotty is an elected delegate to the Navajo Nation Council and represents many communities on the vast reservation. Crotty's goal is to encourage support of survivors of sexual assault. Under her leadership, the Navajo Nation continues to advance initiatives that protect its women and children, as well as its most vulnerable populations. Crotty advocates for community support and increased basic policing She gained national attention for her "Start by Believing" campaign with a "Brief but Spectacular" appearance on the PBS News Hour in 2019. Brief but Spectacular, PBS News Hour, May 16, 2019. (birth year not available).

Leonora "Babsie" Curtin upon her marriage to Y.A. Paloheimo.

Curtin, Leonora "Babsie." One of three generations of Curtin women who influnced Santa Fe's art scene. When her mother died, Leonora "Babsie" Curtin used her vast inherited wealth to establish El Rancho de las Golondrinas outside Santa Fe. After "Babsie" married Finnish diplomat Y.A. Paloheimo, the family began to restore and reconstruct its buildings. Earlier, Babsie founded the Native Market (later to become the Spanish Market) to assist native artisans in selling traditional furniture. Babsie subsequently moved to Washington, DC for a career in linguistics at the Smithsonian Institute specializing in Pueblo Indian dialects. In 1946, she married Paloheimo. The Paloheimos later moved to El Rancho de las Golondrinas to establish a living museum of Spanish Colonial history. Babsie and her mother were founding members of the Spanish Colonial Arts Society and major contributors to the Museum of Spanish Colonial Arts. Babsie was also a major donor to the School of American Research, now the School of Advanced Research. (1903–1990). New Mexico Historic Women Marker Initiative. *Three Wise Women: The Life and Legacy of Eva and the Leonoras.* Women's International Study Center, 2018.

Curtis, Dulcelina. Agriculturalist, farmer, conservationist. Dulcelina Curtis led efforts to control flooding of arroyos in Corrales where a flood-control channel is named in her honor. The first woman appointed to a board of the US Agricultural Stabilization and Conservation District, Curtis received the National Endowment for Soil Conservation Award for New Mexico in 1988. She served on the Corrales Village Council and helped launch many of its civic organizations. *New Mexico Women* called her "a hard-working visionary." Curtis was the first woman appointed to a board of the US Agriculture and Stabilization District. (1904–1995). New Mexico Historic Women Marker Initiative.

Curtis, Natalie. Ethnomusicologist. New York born and bred Natalie Curtis transformed herself into a "new woman" with her move to the Southwest. Ethnologist Elsie Clews Parsons interpreted the term to mean "the woman not yet classified, perhaps not classifiable, the woman new not only to men, but to herself." Curtis followed suit in applying it to herself. Natalie Curtis was one of a small group of women who carried out important ethnological studies in North America at the beginning of the twentieth century. She is remembered for her transcriptions and publication of traditional music of Native American tribes. But it was in New Mexico where Curtis was able to, as she saw it, complete her "unfinished life." That life began with her visits to Arizona in the 1890s; soon she became a seasoned visitor to the Southwest. This, and her innate curiosity, merged with her interest in Native American music. She published *The Indian's Book* in 1907. (1875–1921). *Ladies of the Canyons: A League of Extraordinary Women and Their Adventures in the American Southwest.*

Natalie Curtis.

Dare, Adrienne, PhD. Passionate mathematician, death with dignity advocate. Adrienne Dare is acknowledged for her passion and commitment to the usefulness of a mathematics education, especially for girls. Dare early recognized that one obstacle to learning mathematics was the fear of it. Consequently, Dare worked in her classroom to develop strategies to overcome that fear. Later, she went on to earn a doctorate in mathematics from New Mexico State University. She has worked for many years to increase the number of young women entering professions requiring advanced studies in mathematics and science. Having worked with her mother through the transition from life to death, Dare also has been active in the Death with Dignity movement. (ca. 1950s–). http://www. Death with dignity.

Adrienne Dare and mother.

Davis, Linda. Cowpuncher. With husband Les, Linda Davis operated the 200,000 acre CS Ranch in northern New Mexico near Cimarron. During World War II, women had to run the ranches when their men were off to war, and even young girls were called on to undertake tasks generally off-limits to them. As an example, Davis recalls a particularly nasty stretch of downhill slope which drivers habitually shied away from. "Back then the road was dirt. It was a real challenge to steer a truck of cattle.... My father finally gave me the keys when I was nine years old. He did so only because my foot could finally reach the brake pedal." She is an inductee and director of the National Cowboy Hall of Fame. (1930–). New Mexico Farm & Ranch Heritage Museum. KRQE News at 10. *Albuquerque Journal,* June 16, 2009. https://www.krqe.com/news/new-mexicans-inducted-in-cowboy-hall-of-fame.

Linda Davis, Cowboy Hall of Fame.

Decker, Carol. Worked for "amistad," "comprensión" between cultures. Carol Decker was still teaching Spanish, had just published her latest book, and was building her own website when she died at age eighty-seven. No-one captured Decker's life more succinctly or eloquently than longtime friend and former Santa Fe School Board member Mary Ellen Gonzales, who called Decker "a model about how we can live with people who are different from us." Typical was an early effort called Vecinos (or neighbors) del Norte, guided by the principle of creating community between members of the Santa Fe populations who feared an influx of those they saw as outsiders who would swallow up their indigenous diverse cultures. Decker was the quintessential outsider, the ultimate Yankee. Born on the campus of the prestigious Phillips Academy in Andover, Massachusetts, where her father was a faculty member, she spent her formative years in the East before ultimately swapping its culture for that of Santa Fe and northern New Mexico. Sharing her love for Santa Fe and environs was "one of her most joyful experiences." Before her death, Decker was named one of the New Mexico's Ten Who Made a Difference and a Santa Fe Living Treasure. The Vecinos project is written of lovingly in *Connecting Across Cultures,* published by Sunstone Press. She is also the author of *Pecos Pueblo People Through the Ages* and *The Great Pecos Mission (1540–2000)* from Sunstone Press. (1927–2015). Anne Constable, *Santa Fe New Mexican*, February 25, 2015.

DeHuff, Elizabeth Willis. Contributed to easel painting, encouraged traditional themes. At the Santa Fe Indian School in the 1920s and 1930s, Elizabeth DeHuff encouraged the development of modern easel painting in which she is considered an important contributor. She also urged her students to utilize themes from their tribal heritage, insisting she was present at the "real awakening" of Southwest Indian painting. DeHuff also wrote children's books utilizing Native American folklore and themes. Among them are *Blue-Wings-Flying* and *Tay Tay's Tales*. In writing these and other books, DeHuff was instrumental in documenting Native American folklore and providing authenticity in its the telling. She wrote 65 works in 118 publications (1886–1983). https://ann nolan clark/elizabeth-willis-dehuff.

Denish, Diane D. Voice for the voiceless. The descendant of a long line of public servants in New Mexico, Diane Denish believes holding office allows one to "[g]et connected to peoples' lives and hear their stories. Sometimes, you are the voice for the voiceless and an advocate for those left behind." She was the first woman to be elected lieutenant governor in New Mexico and was subsequently re-elected. (1949–) *Mujeres Valerosas ... meet the extraordinary women of the New Mexico Hispanic Women's Council.*

Diane Denish. Wikipedia

Margretta Dietrich. Wikipedia

Dietrich, Margretta. Indian rights/women's suffrage advocate. Before coming to New Mexico, Margretta Dietrich was president of the Nebraska Women's Suffrage Association and chairman of the state's League of Women Voters. That set the stage for her work in New Mexico. She and her husband first visited Santa Fe in 1921 and in 1927 made New Mexico their permanent home. Dietrich soon became deeply involved in Pueblo and Navajo causes, lobbying against development of dams and exploration in Native American villages. She believed that "even to drill" on Pueblo land might desecrate sacred areas and could destroy an important part of indigenous culture. She became president of the New Mexico Association on Indian Affairs and led it off and on from 1932 until 1952, working for tribes to organize for self-government. Dietrich assisted in inception of the present-day Santa Fe Indian Market, providing weavers with wool and artists with supplies. She aided in furnishing food to the Pueblos during the drought of 1923 and in battling a whooping cough epidemic. During World War II, she befriended New Mexico Native American soldiers, many of whom wrote her from far-flung battlefields. (1881–1961). *New Mexico Recollections.*

Dissette, Mary. Missionary to the Zuni. In 1888, the Presbyterian Board of Home Missions sent Mary Dissette to New Mexico to convert and civilize the people of Zuni Pueblo. She stayed there for almost 12 years, serving as the mission school teacher, then as superintendent of its Industrial School, then as a Bureau of Indian Affairs teacher, then as a nurse during a smallpox epidemic, and finally as a field matron. Dissette worked in various aspects of Indian education for thirty years, teaching near Laguna Pueblo and at Santo Domingo Pueblo in the 1910s, serving as a librarian at the Santa Fe Indian School in the 1920s, and then in Oklahoma before returning to Santa Fe. "Making Savages of Us All: White Women, Pueblo Indians, and the Controversy over Indian Dances in the 1920s." (birth and death dates not available). *Margaret D. Jacobs. A Journal of Women Studies, Vol. 17, No. 3.* (1996), 178-209, University of Nebraska Press.

Sister Katharine Marie Drexel.

Drexel, Sister Katharine Marie. Founded Sisters of the Blessed Sacrament for Indians and Colored People. Sister Katharine Marie Drexel used her considerable personal fortune to fund schools for Native Americans in New Mexico and for African Americans elsewhere. In 1891, Katharine Drexel put behind her a life as a wealthy heiress to become a nun. Her fortune derived from her father's business association with financier J.P. Morgan. In addition to their great wealth, her parents were known for their philanthropy. Having traveled throughout the United States, Drexel was aware of the difficult circumstances faced by Native Americans and African Americans. She wanted to use her wealth to help them. During a trip to Europe in 1887 before entering religious life, she met Pope Leo XIII and asked him to recommend a religious order that could send missionaries to the institutions she was funding. He suggested that Drexel undertake the work herself. In 1889, Drexel entered religious life under the Sisters of Mercy in Pittsburgh, Pennsylvania. With the help of other nuns, she founded the Sisters of the Blessed Sacrament for Indians and Colored People, now known as the Sisters of the Blessed Sacrament. Drexel and fifteen sisters established a school for Native Americans in Santa Fe in 1894. This was followed by other schools throughout the Southwest. Drexel's order also opened many schools for African American children and an institution now known as Xavier University. During her life, she gave $20 million to help people in need. In the 1960s, the Catholic Church began considering Drexel for sainthood. She was beatified in 1988 after the Vatican found that prayers to her had restored a teenager's hearing. In 2000, she was credited with a second cure, and Pope John Paul II canonized her as Saint Katharine Drexel later that same year. (1858–1955). www.katharinedrexelcc.org/patron-st-katharine-drexel.

Durand, Cora. Keeper of the micaceous pottery tradition. Cora Durand kept the micaceous pottery tradition alive for her Picuris Pueblo people and generously shared her knowledge and gifts, leaving behind an important legacy. She began work late in life after holding a variety of jobs, including with the Bureau of Indian Affairs. Durand intended for her work to be used in utilitarian ways rather than as decorative art work. Her greatest legacy is keeping the tradition of her Pueblo's pottery alive. Working with Durand in this effort were Maria Ramita Simbola Martinez and Virginia Duran. (1904–1998). New Mexico Historic Women Marker Initiative.

Bertha Pauline Dutton.

Dutton, Bertha Pauline, PhD. Scholar, educator, administrator. Bertha "Bert" Dutton's career as scholar, educator, and finally as administrator at the Museum of New Mexico covered nearly sixty years. *Women in Education: New Mexico* notes that she "exuded charm and warm personality, combined with good humor and a zest for living." Highlights of her professional life included extensive work excavating pueblos in the Galisteo Basin and founding and directing an education program for the Girl Scouts. Her excavation work earned the affectionate title for its participants as "Dutton's Dirty Diggers." Dutton strove to convince her young charges that they "could be anything they wanted to be." Her mantra was "Do it and do it right!" In an article for *El Palacio*, Leslie Cohen wrote that "Bertha Pauline Dutton changed lives." Dutton's mentor was famed Southwestern archaeologist and anthropologist Edgar Lee Hewett, whom she met while serving as a secretary in the University of New Mexico's archaeology department. Recognizing her potential and ability, Hewitt invited her on a field trip to the Jemez area. As a result, Dutton's career path was fixed. More field trips to South and Central America led to a post as head of the department of ethnology at the University of New Mexico. One of Dutton's abiding research interests was migration patterns between Mesa Verde and the Galisteo Basin. She was a prolific writer (one hundred articles for *El Palacio Magazine*) with publications ranging from scientific journals to popular magazines and to work such as *Sun Father's Way and Indians of the American Southwest.* (1903–1994). "She Taught Us to be Bold," *El Palacio.* 111 (Summer 2006), 34-37.

Stella Dysart.

Dysart, Stella. Woman "wildcatter." In becoming a uranium wildcatter, Stella Dysart accumulated great wealth. It took her thirty years to do so. Dysart held vast uranium properties near Grants, New Mexico. But it was a long way from her days in a San Francisco dressmaking shop where she first entered business. Dysart later became interested in oil properties where she worked alongside men in the oil fields she owned, making a fortune for herself, her investors, and her family. She later acquired and developed the Ambrosia Lake uranium field in New Mexico. Dysart spent her later years in Albuquerque where she shared her wealth with local hospitals and charities—notably those for unwed mothers and their children. (1878–1966). *Notable New Mexico Women. Stella Dysart of Ambrosia Lake.*

Eber, Christine, PhD. Change through weaving. Christine Eber is a professor emerita of anthropology at New Mexico State University and the recipient of the Governor's Award for Service to the People of New Mexico and Mexico. She has conducted research and applied work in the Mexican state of Chiapas for decades through encouragement of Maya women's participation in weaving cooperatives. Eber has focused on the gendered aspects of social change for Maya women in the Zapatista movement, cooperatives, and the Catholic Church. She is a founding member of Weaving for Justice, a volunteer network based in Las Cruces that assisted Maya weavers to sell their products through fair trade and educated consumers about the effects of globalization on indigenous artisans. Eber said she saw this as an opportunity "to give back" for all that the women of Chiapas had given her. Working with them, she said, was the "turning point" of her life. Eber is the author of numerous scholarly works and a novel, *When A Woman Rises*. (1946 -). https://www.christineeber.com. https://anthropology.nmsu.edu/anthropology-faculty/eber. http://www.christineeber.com/about/christine.

Isabel Eckles.
Courtesy of Silver City New Mexico Museum.

Eckles, Isabel. Classroom launchpad for political career. Silver City teacher Isabel Eckles was elected Grant County school superintendent in 1911, taking office just as New Mexico attained statehood. Eckles served as superintendent for seven years, then became registrar at the Normal School (later Western New Mexico University), and served as its acting president for several months. Eckles was elected State Superintendent of Schools in 1922. After two terms in office, she became Superintendent of Schools in Santa Fe for ten years and then completed her career in the Women's Division of the WPA for New Mexico. Eckles was the first woman to head the New Mexico Education Association, served as president of the National Council of Administrative Women in Education, and was appointed by President Calvin Coolidge as the New Mexico representative for Education and Health. (1877–1971). "Coloring Outside the Lines: Empowered women in territorial and early-statehood Silver City," *Desert Exposure*, March 2012.

Grace Edmister.

Edmister, Grace Keenen Thompson. New Mexico's music maker. Grace Edmister was one of the first women in the United States to lead a municipal symphony when she launched the Albuquerque Civic Orchestra in 1932. Edmister also headed the music department at the University of New Mexico, working her way up from piano teacher. She developed New Mexico's public schools' music curriculum and taught at Pueblos where she encouraged many Native Americans into following music careers. "The time is coming," she told New Mexico music educators, "when the chance to learn to make music" will be offered in all public schools on an equal footing with other subjects. All this from someone who had come to New Mexico seeking recovery from tuberculosis; Edmister ended up living ninety-four years. (1890–1984). *Women in Education: New Mexico. Notable New Mexico Women.*

Pauline Eisenstadt.
Courtesy of University of New Mexico Press.

Eisenstadt, Pauline. A foot in both houses. Pauline Eisenstadt has the distinction of serving in both houses of the New Mexico legislature as the title of her autobiography, *A Woman in Both Houses: My Career in New Mexico Politics*, suggests. Eisenstadt believes that what made her successful in a man's world of state politics was her "tenacity and a willingness" to confront men on issues dear to her. Eisenstadt especially cares about prenatal care for women, prevention of child abuse, and ethics. A confrontation with the prevailing male-dominated system in New Mexico politics taught Eisenstadt that "truth can be manipulated by power." She vowed always to fight what she considered to be abuses in the system. (1938–). *A Woman in Both Houses: My Career in New Mexico Politics.*

Eldridge, Mary Louise and Mary E. Raymond. Point of the spear for Methodism in Navajoland. In October of 1891, Mary Louise Eldridge and Mary E. Raymond arrived from Methodist mission headquarters in the East to begin missionary work among the Navajos near Fruitland, New Mexico. The young women were astute enough to know there was another way to introduce Christianity to their new charges rather than first waving a Bible at them. They began providing elementary health care along with offering farm implements and seeds, along with helping in constructing irrigation ditches, among other improvement projects. (birth and death dates not available). *Women in Education: New Mexico.*

Elliott, Erica M., MD. The "Health Detective." Erica Elliott draws from a wide range of disciplines—mainstream and alternative—to treat illness, including those that do not respond to pharmaceutical drugs and other conventional treatments. Upon leaving college, she began teaching on the Navajo reservation. There she learned to speak the language and was accepted into the life and culture of the Navajos. After teaching, Elliott became a sheepherder, living traditionally. Her family believed she would marry into the Diné people and spend the rest of her days with them. But curiosity drew her to a deeper understanding of other indigenous cultures. Elliott joined the Peace Corps with an assignment to the Ecuadorian Andes where she taught Quechua-speaking children to speak Spanish. When Elliott returned home, she learned that medicine was her destiny. She became a well-respected, conventional, mainstream, family-practice doctor in Santa Fe. After a few years, a serious illness sidelined her. In her pursuit of wellness, Elliott dove deeply into environmental medicine and learned some important pieces of the health puzzle that had been absent in her previous medical training. Ultimately, she used what she had learned to facilitate healing in her own medical practice. Her book, *Medicine and Miracles in the High Desert*, recounts her struggles in improvising health care in a bare-bones clinic in Cuba, New Mexico. *Medicine and Miracles in the High Desert: My Life Among the Navajo People*. Prescriptions for a Healthy House. David Steinberg *Albuquerque Journal*, May 26, 2019.

Florence Hawley Ellis.

Ellis, Florence Hawley. Discovered the value of tree-ring dating. Florence Hawley Ellis was born in a Mexican mining camp in 1906. Her first memories were of marching rebels, burned bridges, and flights into the hills. Her second was of becoming interested as a young girl in the ancient ruins near her father's mining locations in Arizona. Her future in fieldwork was thus fixed. She took two degrees at the University of Arizona and was a member of its first class of tree-ring studies. Ellis conducted archeological and ethnological research in New Mexico and throughout the Southwest and undertook some of the first dendrochronological research in the mid-twentieth century. A passionate teacher, she encouraged her students to think for themselves and to work hard for what they wanted. As an exemplar, she often taught course loads many times heavier than her male colleagues at the University of New Mexico. Although faced with many challenges and discriminated against for her gender, Ellis persevered and became a strong influence both for her students and for other women in her field. A museum is named for her at Ghost Ranch in Abiquiu, New Mexico. (1906–1991). *Notable New Mexico Women. Women in Education: New Mexico. Buried Treasures: Famous and Unusual Gravesites in New Mexico History.*

Ellis, Magnolia Yoakum. Magnificent Magnolia. Patients claimed to have a feeling of electricity when Magnolia Ellis touched them at her clinic in Hot Springs (now Truth or Consequences), New Mexico. She was known for her unique psychic and healing abilities. Magnolia Ellen Yoakum got her first name from her Cherokee father, who named her after the first tree his wife saw after their daughter's birth. From childhood, she had the ability to see the future. This gift would later help her as a healer. To support her family, Magnolia became a teacher. While traveling during a break from teaching, she met and married C. P. Ellis, but the marriage did not last. After her divorce, she relocated to Hot Springs to start her clinic and take advantage of the town's hot springs. (1893–1974). New Mexico Historic Women Marker Initiative.

Estrada, Emma. *Partera* for three decades. The practice of midwifery was essential to the birthing process in New Mexico for many years. In a large, mostly rural state with few doctors, midwives—or *parteras*—assisted thousands of women in giving birth. After the University of New Mexico's medical school opened in 1961, the state began to train and certify midwives. She became the first licensed *partera* in New Mexico and worked with doctors to assure the best medical care. Emma delivered more than seven hundred babies during an era when mothers had no choice but to deliver at home. She is remembered for her quiet confidence and devotion. (1904–1988). New Mexico Historic Women Marker Initiative.

Farquhar, Myrtle Attaway. Inspiration for African-American students. Myrtle Attaway Farquhar, arriving in New Mexico from Texas with a master's degree and a dedication to teaching African-American students, accepted a position in 1943 at the segregated Booker T. Washington School in Hobbs. She inspired students to pursue higher education, and she and her husband helped finance at least ten of them through college. The Farquhars had no children but supported and encouraged children of their own race. Her former students recall Myrtle as strict and demanding excellence. After school hours, she tutored pupils around her kitchen table. When some of her students left for college, they departed with the semester's cash pinned inside their clothing. (1900–1972). New Mexico Historic Women Marker Initiative. *Bridges: New Mexico Black Women, 1900–1950.*

Eva Scott Fényes.

Fényes, Eva Scott. Progenitor of influential New Mexico women. Eva Scott Fényes created artistic and photographic records of New Mexico's missions and adobe buildings. But she was much more. She was the mother of Leonora Scott Muse and grandmother of Leonora "Babsie" Curtin Paloheimo, all supportive of Santa Fe's cultural life. Fényes was the daughter of a wealthy New York publisher who married Marine Corps General W.E. Muse, father of Leonora Curtin. Scott's second husband was Hungarian nobleman Adelbert Fényes. She later became interested in cultural preservation. (1849–1930). New Mexico Historic Women Marker Initiative. *Three Wise Women: The Life and Legacy of Eva and the Two Leonoras.*

Erna Fergusson.

Fergusson, Erna. New Mexican literary icon. Born to a wealthy and prominent Albuquerque family, Erna Fergusson documented the culture and history of her native state for four decades. Her work popularized the Land of Enchantment and promoted tourism. Among her important works are *Dancing Gods: Indian Ceremonials of New Mexico and Arizona* (still timely and relevant), *New Mexico: A Pageant of Three Peoples*, and *Erna Fergusson's Albuquerque*. Southwestern literary critic Lawrence Clark Powell said *Dancing Gods* remains "still the best of all books about the Indian ceremonials of New Mexico and Arizona." Fergusson also was successful as a businesswoman and tour operator assisting Fred Harvey in organizing a group of attractive and knowledgeable young women to lead his Indian Detour excursions to Southwestern cultural and historic attractions. Always an observer and commentator on her state's Native people, Fergusson once noted that the idea of the "Changing Indian" had taken the place of the "Vanishing Indian" in the collective mindset of the American public. Acknowledged as part of the Southwest Renaissance, she co-founded the

Albuquerque Historical Society. Biographer Don Bullis called her the "Grand Dame of New Mexico Letters." (1888–1964). *Dancing Gods: Indian Ceremonials of New Mexico and Arizona. New Mexico, A Pageant of Three Peoples. Erna Fergusson's Albuquerque. Notable New Mexico Women.*

Fitzpatrick, Mildred Gunn Kimbrough, EdD. Educator. Mildred Fitzpatrick was a leader at all levels of education in New Mexico during several decades, serving as teacher and subsequently as administrator with the State Department of Education. Fitzpatrick, a nationally recognized educator, was a classroom teacher, rural school supervisor and principal, university professor and Director of Elementary Education for the New Mexico State Department of Education. She was the author and co-author of textbooks and workbooks and a former president of the New Mexico Education Association. She co-authored *New Mexico for Young People* with husband, George Fitzpatrick, editor of *New Mexico Magazine.* (1911–1984). Find A Grave. *Notable New Mexico Women.*

Fleck, Marion Rohovec, PhD. Nurse and educator. Marion Fleck taught at Albuquerque and Belen High Schools until World War II motivated her to become a nurse. She earned a master's degree from the Yale School of Nursing, eventually returning to New Mexico to pursue careers in nursing and education. She was Director of Health and Nursing Services in Albuquerque Public Schools from 1957 to 1974 and earned a doctorate in 1970 from the University of New Mexico (UNM). Fleck and a colleague developed the plan and curriculum for the College of Nursing at UNM, secured funding, and shepherded the College of Nursing into reality. She served on the Board of Trustees of the American Nursing Foundation and the American School Health Association. Among her honors are the New Mexico State Distinguished Service Award. In 2002, Dr. Fleck was named by March of Dimes as a Legend in Nursing. She was married to Martin W. Fleck, PhD, UNM Biology Professor. For their contributions to the community, the couple received the Presbyterian Healthcare Foundation Award. (1917–2016). *Albuquerque Journal,* August 28, 2016.

Kathy Flynn.

Flynn, Kathy. Preserver of the New Deal Legacy. After a lifetime of service to New Mexico in diverse fields, Kathy found a new calling—identifying, documenting, and preserving New Deal efforts in New Mexico and elsewhere. That led to birth of the state and national New Deal Preservation Associations and her role as Chief Executive Officer. A shared goal is education about the New Deal projects originated by President Franklin D. Roosevelt at the height of the Great Depression to provide employment for the country's out-of-work and to shore up the nation's failing infrastructure. Representative of work was her participation in the Ken Burns documentary *The Roosevelts: An Intimate History*. As a well-respected national expert on New Deal buildings, projects, and artwork she had collected a huge personal collection of visual images she made accessible to Burns. She has been named a Santa Fe Living Tresure and "Ten Who Made a Difference" by the *Santa Fe New Mexican*. Flynn has written three books on the New Deal, including *Public Art and Architecture in New Mexico, 1933–1943, A Guide to the New Deal Legacy*, published by Sunstone Press. (1936–). Sunstone Press and *Santa Fe New Mexican.*

Foraker, Mary Louise. Strong advocate. In December 1951, Mary Foraker became the first classroom teacher elected president of the New Mexico Education Association (NMEA). Foraker, a career classroom teacher in Albuquerque, was active at all levels in advancing her profession in New Mexico. She was vice president of NMEA before assuming the presidency. Foraker shared her thoughts on involvement and participation at the 2nd Council on unified membership of the National Education Association. "It is in the local," she said, "that ideas are born, leaders are developed, good public relations are fostered, and...[members] acquire a broad professional outlook...." Foraker added that if the NEA "did nothing more" than conduct research, defend the profession against unjust attacks, and upgrade the profession "it would be worth much more than the [annual] $5 membership fee." (1903–1989). National Education Association-New Mexico. *Women in Education: New Mexico.*

Elizabeth Forster. Bing.

Forster, Elizabeth. Encouraged Navajo to integrate medical traditions. Public Health nurse Elizabeth Forster and noted Southwestern photographer Laura Gilpin were close but pursued independent lives and careers, Gilpin's the more notable. Their lives and relationship are related in the novel *Land Beyond Maps* and *Denizens of the Desert: A Tale in Words* and *Pictures of Life Among the Navaho Indians: The Letters of Elizabeth W. Forster/Photographs by Laura Gilpin*. As a nurse working on the reservation, Forster encouraged the Navajo to use their traditional healing methods in tandem with Western medicine. She was innovative in that she encouraged the Navajo to use their rituals and saw them as complementary parts of the healing process. (1886–1972). *Denizens of the Desert: A Tale in Words* and *Pictures of Life Among the Navaho Indians: The Letters of Elizabeth W. Forster/Photographs by Laura Gilpin.*

Franks, M. Edythe. Albuquerque civil rights activist. Edythe Franks strove to shine the spotlight on racial discrimination and to eliminate it in the Albuquerque workplace. In the 1930s and 1940s, she did so in the

Albuquerque public schools and then later with Mountain Bell Corporation which resulted in employment of its first two African-American telephone switchboard operators. She served on the board of the National Council of Negro Women and as president of Albuquerque chapter of the NAACP. (birth and death dates not available). *Noteworthy Black Women of New Mexico.*

Evelyn Fisher Frisbie.

Frisbie, Evelyn Fisher, MD.. Early medical practitioner. A 1902 graduate of the Illinois College of Medicine, Frisbie arrived in New Mexico in 1908. From her parents' homestead near Wagon Mound, she set up practice, often riding horseback to see patients as far away as twenty five miles. In 1911, Frisbie moved to Albuquerque, where she was the only woman among the twenty five physicians then serving the town's 20,000 inhabitants. Frisbie practiced medicine in New Mexico for fifty four years—first as a general practitioner, then as an obstetrician/gynecologist. She earned the confidence of her patients and the respect of fellow physicians, who in 1916 elected her president of the New Mexico Medical Society as the first woman head of a state medical society in the country. Frisbie's approach to health care was both generous and personal. She was said to have never turned away a person in need of care. After helping Congregational Church missionaries set up clinics during the 1920s in the Spanish-speaking communities of Cubero, San Mateo, and Bluewater, she continued to make monthly calls there. As medical advisor to women at the University of New Mexico during the 1930s and staff member of the Los Griegos Clinic during the 1940s, she continued her community service in addition to a private practice. Frisbie also worked closely with the Masonic Shrine in its crippled children program and was the first chairman of cancer detection clinics for Bernalillo County. A woman of innate culture and refinement, she demonstrated leadership not only in her profession, but in the community as well. Despite her breeding, she was frank in a woman-to-woman fashion when Frances Minerva Nunnery (see Frances Minerva Nunnery) consulted her about birth control. "Keep your feet in a bucket," was the blunt response. When Nunnery told the doctor she was going to become a rancher, Frisbie added "That's all right. You can't do anything else, either, when you're straddling a horse." (1873–1965). American Association of University Women-New Mexico. "Evelyn Fisher Frisbie."

Gallegos, Fedelina. A pair of proud "firsts." New Mexico Representatives Fedelina Gallegos and **Porfirria Hidalgo Saiz**, who both served in the New Mexico House of Representatives from 1931 to 1932, were the first Hispanic female legislators in the United States. Gallegos was a Republican, Saiz a Democrat. *New Mexico Women Legislators Since Statehood*. Center for American Women and Politics.(Death and birth dates unknown).

Gallegos Fuente, Carlotta and Monica. Ranched 375,000 acres at Gallegos, New Mexico. The sisters married a pair of brothers, Francisco and Emeterio, on the same day on November 27, 1872. Monica Gallegos operated a general store and saloon and issued script in her name. When infamous outlaw Black Jack Ketchum raided the ranch in 1890, Monica shot him in the arm. Monica and Carlotta built a school and the Church of the Immaculate Conception, furnished with large Italian statues. Their vision ensured economic and social stability in Gallegos. In doing so, they helped establish Harding County. Carlotta Gallegos (1857–1936) and Monica Gallegos (1851–1909). New Mexico Historic Women Marker Initiative.

Garcia, Estella R. Teacher, fabric artist. Estella Garcia taught colcha embroidery for the Federal Arts Program at tiny Melrose, New Mexico, during the Great Depression, thus passing on an important art to scores of deserving Anglo and Hispanic women and providing income for their families. Their work in the form of theater curtains, wall hangings, and seat coverings enriched institutions around the state. The facility was considered to be located in the smallest town in New Mexico to have such a federal art center. Garcia's work and that of her students was exhibited at many New Deal art exhibitions around the United States. They also produced a number of theater curtains, including for the Albuquerque

Little Theater, Melrose High School, and Carrie Tingley Hospital in Truth or Consequences. (birth and death dates unavailable.) New Mexico Historic Women Marker Initiative.

Elizabeth Garrett.

A Place of Her Own: The Story of Elizabeth Garrett.

Garrett, Elizabeth. New Mexico's First Lady of Song. Elizabeth Garrett's story is related in *A Place of Her Own: The Story of Elizabeth Garrett* by Ruth K Hall. The title refers to the home designed and built for her in Roswell where Elizabeth lived out her latter years. Born blind on a remote ranch in Lincoln County, New Mexico, this indomitable, self-reliant woman substituted her remaining senses for her lack of sight to become a nationally recognized singer and composer. Elizabeth had to travel to far-off Austin, Texas, for her education at a school for the visually impaired. Later she went to the Midwest and East for further voice training and subsequently to entertain troops and Red Cross patients in World War I. When Garrett could no longer rely on herself for independence, she turned to seeing eye dogs. At a time when women were still trying to assert themselves in society, Garrett followed her own path. As one observer remarked, "She neither sought nor accepted pity but, using her own resources, created a life and a philosophy that became a source of wonder to all who knew her." Born to frontier sheriff Pat Garrett, who fatally shot Billy the Kid, and a Hispanic mother, Elizabeth grew up speaking English and Spanish and experienced the lawless days of frontier New Mexico. Elizabeth once said "My father tried to bring peace and harmony to our county with his guns; I would like to do my part with music." She transcended her lack of sight and was able to write of New Mexico's wonders and natural beauty without ever having seen them. She wrote the New Mexico state song, "O Fair New Mexico," represented the state at the San Diego Exposition in 1915, was an early proponent of women's liberation, and served on the Board of Regents for the New Mexico School for the Blind. She developed friendships with many notable figures of her time, including Helen Keller, who called her "a fellow companion in the dark." (1885–1947). *Notable New Mexico Women. A Place of Her Own: The Story of Elizabeth Garett. Buried Treasures: Famous and Unusual Gravesites in New Mexico History.*

Fabiola Cabeza de Baca Gilbert.
Courtesy of the C' de Baca Family.
"Aunt Fabie" (in glasses) with Mrs. Pancho Villa.

Gilbert, Fabiola Cabeza de Baca. Educator, nutritionist, activist, writer. As a recognized authority on traditional foods, Fabiola Gilbert Cabeza de Baca published *Historic Cookery*, describing New Mexico cuisine, and *The Good Life, New Mexico Traditions and Food.* Gilbert observed that "New Mexico is a land of changes. Its blue skies of morning may be red skies of evening." So too, she noted, have there been changes in its food habits. As with its people, the state's food is a product of "past and present—an amalgamation of Indian, Spanish, Mexican, and American." She was an unflagging advocate of healthy food and nutrition for New Mexicans.

Over her thirty year career in education, her teaching philosophy was encapsulated as: "Discipline is obtained with love." A gifted linguist, Gilbert was fluent in Spanish, English, and the native Pueblo languages Tewa and Tiwa. Perhaps her greatest contribution was, in her words, "telling the story of the New Mexico Hispanos [striving] for existence on the Llano Estacado [the Staked Plains of New Mexico and Texas]," which she did in her highly entertaining memoir *We Fed Them Cactus*. The title comes from the drought years when her rancher-father was forced to burn off the spines of cactus before feeding the succulent to his cattle to keep them alive. The book examines the history and settling of the Llano before the advent of the Americanos. "[A] great debt," she writes "is owed to the brave, pioneer women [of whom she was one] who ventured into the cruel life of the plains, far from contact with the outside world." The Llano is a plateau of 60,000 square miles extending from the Canadian River, rising in New Mexico's Sangre de Christo Mountains, southward four hundred miles. (1894–1991). *The Good Life, New Mexico Traditions and Food. We Fed Them Cactus.* New Mexico Historic Women Marker Initiative. *Women in Education: New Mexico.*

Gill, Inez Bushner. Fiscal expertise impressive. A member of the original staff of the New Mexico Legislative Council Service upon its founding in 1951, Inez Gill impressed lawmakers with her fiscal expertise. She was an acknowledged fiscal analyst and helped establish the Legislative Finance Committee and the Department of Finance and Administration. Gill has been called two of the "most important and influential women in New Mexico state government." Former New Mexico governor Garrey Carruthers said, "She stands with the finest of governors, senators, congressmen and all other public servants in terms of contributions to our state." Supported by family wealth, Gill retired from state service at the age of forty-six to devote herself to charitable pursuits (1918–1982). New Mexico Historic Women Marker Initiative.

Laura Gilpin. Bing.

Gilpin, Laura. American Southwest in her lens. Laura Gilpin's starkly beautiful photographs of the American Southwest helped others "see through her eyes and understand what she considered the beating heart of the natural world," writes Beverly West in *More Than Petticoats: Remarkable New Mexico Women*. Gilpin believed that many photographers had an "impulse to record a scene [often failing] to realize that what they wish to do is record the emotion felt upon viewing that scene...a mere photograph in no way reflects that emotion." In 1924, Gilpin made her first major visit to Taos, San Ildefonso, and Laguna Pueblos and later to the Navajo Reservation in Arizona. Martha Sandweiss writes in *Laura Gilpin: An Enduring Grace* that Gilpin wanted "to document Navajo life, but to do so in a way that did not disguise her own fascination with [them] or compromise her own high pictorial standards." Gilpin's honors began to accumulate when in 1930 she was named an associate of the Royal Photographic Society of Great Britain. At the same time, the Library of Congress purchased some of her work. Gilpin's *The Enduring Navaho* has been called "a classic in photojournalism." A lesser-known but equally intriguing Gilpin book is *The Pueblos: A Camera Chronicle*, published in 1921—consisting of dozens of stunning black-and-white photos mostly from New Mexico accompanied by brief descriptions supplied by Gilpin covering twenty years, commencing with her self-described "soft focus" period. Gilpin spent her declining years wheelchair-bound in Santa Fe, brought about, as she said, "by lugging an eight by ten camera over too many mountains." She left behind an impressive artistic legacy from someone who raised turkeys in her native Colorado to pay for photography school. (1891–1979). *More Than Petticoats: Remarkable New Mexico Women. Laura Gilpin: An Enduring Grace. The Enduring Navaho.* New Mexico Historic Women Marker Initiative. *Notable New Mexico Women.*

Esther Schiff Wittfogel Goldfrank.

Goldfrank, Esther Schiff Wittfogel. A rarity in her field. Esther Goldfrank essentially was self-educated in anthropology. Although she never received a degree in anthropology, Goldfrank graduated from Barnard College in 1918 with a bachelor's degree in economics. She began soon after as a secretary to well-known anthropologist Franz Boas at Columbia University. Despite her lack of academic credentials in anthropology, she made significant contributions to the study of the Pueblo people of New Mexico. Anthropologist Elsie Clews Parsons underwrote her salary and expenses. Accompanied to the Southwest by Boas and Parsons, Goldfrank began her fieldwork by collecting recipes from a Laguna Pueblo woman in June 1920. For the next two seasons, she accompanied Boas to Cochiti Pueblo, where she wrote that her "helpers were a group of women—by and large it was a woman's party." She wrote *The Social and Ceremonial Organization of Cochiti* (1927) based on her collaborative efforts with Carolyn Quintana, mother of the now-famous potter Helen Cordero. Esther coined the name "Papa Franz" for Boas on the trip to Laguna in 1920, and the term gradually caught on among insiders, both men and women, in the anthropology department. Esther interrupted her scientific career in 1922 to marry Walter S. Goldfrank, a widower with three sons. Esther had a daughter in 1924 and did not resume coursework at Columbia until thirteen years later following her husband's death in 1935. Goldfrank married again in 1940 to Karl Wittfogel. Goldfrank wrote several essays on the importance of irrigation for Pueblo organization and ceremonial life. (1896–1997). *Daughters of the Desert.* Esther Schiff Goldfrank/Jewish Women's Archives.

Gonzales, María Dolores, PhD. Early leader in New Mexico bilingual and bicultural education. María Gonzales developed educational material for students in New Mexico and Latin America and trained teachers in its use. Born in Pecos, New Mexico, "Lola" taught in the area for many years and at the University of New Mexico. She held a master's degree from Columbia University in New York and a doctorate from Pennsylvania State University. Lola believed children should learn in both English and Spanish because she wanted them to know and respect both cultures. She also worked to preserve the traditions of the New Mexico Hispanic people. (1917–1975). New Mexico Historic Women Marker Initiative.

Goodacre, Glenna Maxey. *Sculpture extolled adopted home state of New Mexico.* Born, raised, and educated in West Texas, Goodacre moved to Santa Fe in later years and soon became a celebrated member of its arts scene. A smaller replica of her Vietnam Women's Memorial is installed at the Vietnam Veterans Memorial Park in Angel Fire. The Albuquerque Art and History Museum Foundation named her a "Notable New Mexican," calling her an extraordinary New Mexican who had contributed to the public good. Her portrait hangs in its museum. Former Governor Bill Richardson appointed her to the State Quarter Design Committee to develop a U.S. Quarter representing New Mexico. The appointment led to her design of the obverse of the Sacagawea dollar that entered circulation in 2000. (1939–2020).

Grant, Blanche Chloe. Illustrator, landscape painter, author, and editor. Blanche Grant is known for her murals, paintings, and books on the Southwest. One source says she spent as much time on writing as she did on painting. Her books include *Taos Indians*, *Taos Today* and *The Story of Taos.* Subject matter for her art included the landscape and residents of the Taos area. She also edited the *Taos News.* Grant produced murals for the New Mexico Institute of Technology (then New Mexico Tech) and the Taos Presbyterian Church. The murals are no long extant. Grant studied at Vassar College, the Pennsylvania Academy of Fine Arts, and the School of the Museum of Fine Arts in Boston. By 1914, she had established herself as a magazine illustrator and landscape painter. In 1916, she began teaching at the University of Nebraska. In 1920, after returning from a brief hiatus to France, she settled in Taos where she remained until her death. She was also a member the Taos Art Association. (1874–1948).

Gray, Etha. New Mexico communications pioneer. Etha Gray broke the color barrier in television in Albuquerque when she became the first African-American woman to work as news editor for Channel 13. After leaving television, Gray established and became editor of *Four-Star News* in Albuquerque, designed to provide news for the city's minority community. Gray also trained minorities in the print media. (birth and death dates unavailable). *Noteworthy Black Women of New Mexico.*

Gregg, Elinor R.N. "Helper Woman." Elinor Delight Gregg, RN., the first Supervisor of Nurses for the Indian Service, led an independent woman's life of adventure, frustration, triumphs, and personal commitment to caring. Her stories tell of miles traveled through World War l, on Indian reservations, in Washington, DC., and all the journeys between. After nursing with the Red Cross in the trenches of France in WWI, she returned home and began serving with the Sioux on the Rosebud and Pine Ridge Sioux reservations of South Dakota. It was they who gave her the affectionate name "Helper Woman." Throughout her life from factory nurse to the halls of power was one of service. The book is a thoroughly researched true biography set within a fictional relationship between Elinor Gregg and its authors, two University of New Mexico nursing students, in the summer of 1966. (1886–1970). *A Stone for Every Journey. Traveling the Life of Elinor Gregg, R.N.* Sunstone Press, 2004.

Green, Carol Begay. Adapted braille for the Navajo. As a teacher of the blind and visually impaired for the Farmington schools and herself impaired, Carol Begay Green has adapted braille for the Navajo language. Green developed vision problems as a child and lost sight in her left eye at age thirteen. Surgery in her right eye led to further decline in her vision. In 2009, she learned how to read and write braille. With the Navajo language being taught in schools and in some cases being a requirement for students to apply for college scholarships, Green wanted blind and visually impaired students to have a fair opportunity. "I thought if I am going to develop it [braille] for myself, then I might as well share it so these children have that opportunity. The same as their peers," she said. (birth date unavailable.) *Farmington Daily Times*, January 4, 2014.

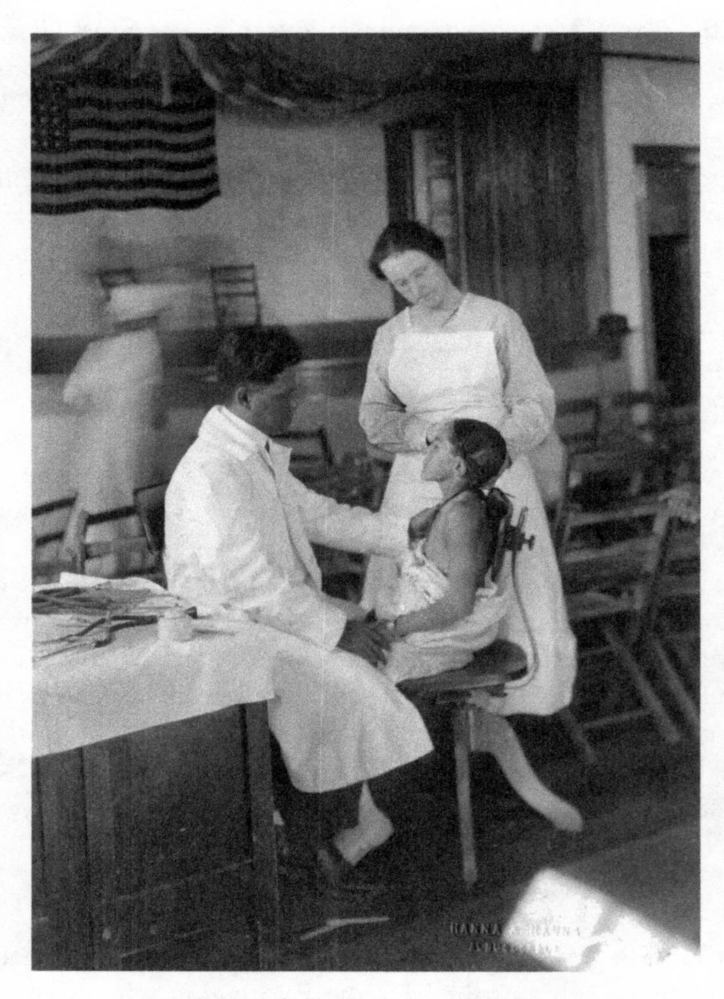

Myrtle Greenfield, Myrtle Greenfield Papers,
University of New Mexico Health Sciences Laboratory and Information Center.

Greenfield, Myrtle. Health services leader. Myrtle Greenfield, trained as a bacteriologist in her native Kansas, came to New Mexico as Director of the New Mexico Public Health Laboratory. It was a post she was to hold for the next thirty-six years. Greenfield might have wondered about having swapped her previous job with the much better equipped United

States Public Health Service for her new quarters in a single room at the Chemistry Department at the University of New Mexico. But, under her supervision, the humble quarters grew into a modern, fully functioning facility with a mobile lab, eventually processing half a million specimens a year. One telling observation went like this: "[s]he ran her laboratory with an iron fist, did it right, and insisted on quality results in the entire operation." Greenfield was active in many professional organizations during her career. She chaired the American Public Health Association and was director of both the New Mexico and National Tuberculosis Association. The University of New Mexico awarded her an honorary doctorate in 1953. Retirement in 1955 afforded her the opportunity to write *A History of Public Health in New Mexico*, published by the University of New Mexico Press in 1962. (1884–1967). Myrtle Greenfield Papers, New Mexico Health Historical Collection, the University of New Mexico Health Sciences Laboratory and Information Center.

Isabella Selmes Ferguson King Greenway.

Greenway, Isabella Selmes Ferguson King. Friend of the mighty, activist. Although Isabella Selmes Ferguson Greenway King gained national prominence in Arizona, she sharpened her political teeth in New Mexico. While Isabella is best known as Arizona's first congresswoman (1933-1936), she got her start in politics polling voters in Grant County, New Mexico, to determine their interest in a presidential run by her longtime friend Theodore Roosevelt. Isabella also was a confidante of Eleanor Roosevelt. Her life in New Mexico began when she and her first husband, Robert Ferguson, arrived in Silver City in November of 1910, renting a cottage outside town. Ferguson suffered from tuberculosis and had to remain isolated. Before long, Isabella's contacts, in addition to her own efforts, led to her being named head of the Women's Land Army for New Mexico, which was an organization of women who assumed the roles of men who had gone to fight in World War I. Isabella called it "potato patriotism." Additional public service included chairing the state's Land Service Committee as well as serving on the State Labor and Reconstruction Board, and the Grant County Board of Education. Isabella's political involvement likely began soon after meeting Isabel Eckles, who was to have a profound effect on her public service sensibilities. All this time, Isabella was trying to find her way in addition to nursing her husband. She hoped the dry climate would improve his health. It did not. After Ferguson's death, Isabella married General John Greenway. He later died of a blood clot. Her last husband was Harry O. King. Part of her story is told in *The New York Times*. "Once more the path of Mrs. Isabella Greenway, by reason of her election as the first woman representative in congress from Arizona, has crossed the Roosevelt path. Her political adversaries say that her overwhelming triumph in the [Arizona congressional] election...was due to her close friendship with the President and Mrs. Roosevelt. They forget her strenuous campaign. She flew up and down the state talking to cattlemen, miners, farmers, bankers, and citizens...[meanwhile] her advisers, secretaries, and pilots drooped under the schedule." (1886–1953). *Isabella Greenway: An Enterprising Woman. Lest We Forget: World War I and New Mexico. The New York Times*, October 22, 1933.

Michelle Lujan Grisham. Office of the Governor, State of New Mexico.

Grisham, Michelle Lujan. Two firsts in elective office. Michelle Grisham is a lawyer and politician serving as the 32nd Governor of New Mexico. She previously represented New Mexico's 1st Congressional District in the United States House of Representatives from 2013 to 2018. On November 6, 2018, she became the first Democratic woman elected governor of New Mexico, as well as the first Democratic Latina elected state chief executive in the United States. She has undergraduate and law degrees from the University of New Mexico, has adult children, and is caretaker for her mother. (1959–). (https://www.governor.state.nm.us/our-leadership/governor/

Gusdorf, Bertha Ferse. Stranger in a strange land. Bertha Gusdorf was born of middle-class Jewish parents in a village of central Germany where she attended school. In 1878 she followed her new husband to what she must have considered to be the wilds of New Mexico, the village of Rancho de Taos. There she was confronted with learning two new languages—English and Spanish—while serving as helpmate to her husband and as the mother of two daughters. Her husband owned a large flour mill and mercantile store and was president of the First State Bank of Taos. Upon his death, Bertha was elected a director, then president. She also oversaw some 12,000 acres of land. (1860–1946). Library of Congress. lcweb2.loc.gov/mss/wpalh1/18/1811/18110104/18110104.pdf.

Debra Haaland

Haaland, Debra. New Mexico Native American Member of Congress, cabinet member. An attorney and active worker in the New Mexico Democratic Party, Deb Haaland was one of two Native women elected to Congress in 2018. In 2021 she became United States Secretary of the Interior, thus becoming the first Native American to hold a cabinet position. Haaland is an enrolled citizen of the Laguna Pueblo and is a 35th generation New Mexican. She has degrees from the University of California at Los Angeles and the University of New Mexico. Both parents served in the military. Her mother is a Native American, her father a Norwegian American. He is a recipient of the Silver Star. (1960–). *Albuquerque Journal*, November 27, 2018.

Hall, Jane Hamilton, PhD. Helped develop the US atomic energy program. A physicist, Jane Hall joined the Los Alamos Scientific Laboratory as part of the team that designed and developed the world's first plutonium-fueled neutron reactor on the Manhattan Project during World War II. She remained at the laboratory after the war and became assistant director in 1958. She was secretary of the General Advisory Committee of the Atomic Energy Commission from 1956 until 1959 and its first woman member from 1966 until 1972. (1915–1981). Wikipedia. *Notable New Mexico Women.*

Hanners, LaVerne. Professor and author. LaVerne Hanners grew up on a northeastern New Mexico cattle ranch. She provides a concise and vivid picture, conveying both realism and a sense of place in *Girl on a Pony.* The book has been called "a gritty, humorous, unflinching account" of coming of age in the isolated Valley of the Dry Cimarron near the Oklahoma border between the two world wars. Hanners, who became a Professor of English at the University of Arkansas, employed earthy language evocative of the cowboy milieu in which she grew up to provide a picture of a time gone by. (1921–1998). *Girl on a Pony.*

Helen Hardin.

Hardin, Helen. An American painter first and foremost. Although Helen Hardin achieved national and international acclaim, she wanted to be acknowledged as an American painter rather than a Native-American artist. Her biography, *A Straight Line Curved,* tells the story of this driven, sometimes edgy but always funny, conflicted, competitive woman, who had a nearly lifelong adversarial relationship with her mother—the equally well-known Pablita Velarde. Hardin's father was an Anglo law enforcement professional whose duties took him to Colombia and Guatemala. There Hardin showed her art and won acclaim. She believed fantasy was important to being an artist: "You have to be where you aren't. My imagination is the soul of my work." Hardin died of cancer less than two weeks after her 41st birthday. As the end approached, she expressed "a great need to be remembered." She blended her Catholic faith and her Pueblo heritage in saying, "It's almost as if there is a great pueblo in the sky." (1943–1984). *A Straight Line Curved. Changing Woman: The Life and Art of Helen Hardin.*

Betty Harris. Wikipedia.

Harris, Betty, PhD. Chemist, researcher, inventor. Betty Harris's interest in chemistry stems from her girlhood. She obtained a bachelor of science degree from Southern University and a master's degree, both in chemistry, from Atlanta University. Both schools are historically Black institutions. Harris began work as a visiting staff member at the Los Alamos National Laboratory (LANL). After gaining exposure to research, she decided to become a research chemist and earned her doctorate from the University of New Mexico. Returning to LANL as a research chemist, Harris worked in hazardous waste treatment and environmental restoration facilities that were contaminated with energetic materials such as propellants and explosives. She eventually became a noted expert in the chemistry of explosives. She worked with the Girl Scouts to develop a chemistry badge similar to the chemistry merit badge for Boy Scouts. Through her research, Harris obtained a patent for her invention of a spot test for identifying explosives in a field environment. (1940–). www.Blackinventor.com.

Judith Harris.

Harris, Judith. Worker for African-American causes. Judith Harris graduated from the State University of New York at Potsdam as a violin major. She taught instrumental music near Syracuse, New York, for more than twenty years. After moving to Albuquerque, Harris involved herself in various African-American causes such as the Sickle Cell Council of New Mexico, which she headed for many years, and Big Brothers/Big Sisters. She was described as "the epitome of gentleness and charm." (1942–2010). *Albuquerque Journal*, June 20, 2010.

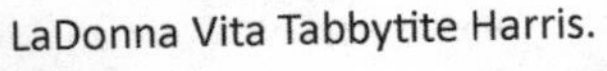
LaDonna Vita Tabbytite Harris.

Harris, LaDonna Vita Tabbytite Link between Indian Country and Washington. LaDonna Vita Tabbytite Harris is a Comanche social activist and politician, who has lived in Albuquerque for nearly fifty years. There she founded Americans for Indian Opportunity. Harris ran for vice president in the 1980 US presidential election, the first Native American woman to do so. She faced bigotry as a child. When she came home sobbing after someone made a racial slur, her grandmother told her, "Bless their hearts, they just don't know better." She entered political life upon marrying fellow Oklahoman Fred Harris, who was elected US Senator. In Washington, LaDonna transitioned into being a Congressional wife but also as a principled, devoted advocate for Native Americans using her political and social status to lobby for change. Fred Harris served in the Senate at a time when Native Americans were expected either to live in the shadows or to assimilate. Native communities faced crippling poverty and unemployment. LaDonna chose diplomacy. "I was as radical as [others of her race], but I had a different style." Harris worked to cut through what she described as a patronizing attitude in Washington. At the direction of President Lyndon B. Johnson, she developed a program to educate lawmakers and officials about Native American tribes and their relationship with the US government. After her husband left office, the couple moved to New Mexico but divorced a few years later. LaDonna has continued in politics and Native advocacy. She has sat on advisory boards for five presidents and helped push through a bill that returned sacred land from the federal government to the Taos Pueblo people. (1931–). *Santa Fe New Mexican*. Sarah Halasz Graham. March 24, 2019.

Harvey Girls. The face of Fred Harvey along the Santa Fe Railroad. These women were the waitresses in Fred Harvey's upscale restaurants that he opened on the Santa Fe Railroad's stops. Harvey Girls have been hailed as contributors to the American story. Subtitles of the many books about the Harvey Girls reveal different, although equally accurate, themes of who they were and what they did. Consequently, it is nearly impossible to select a single woman to write about. One underlying idea is "Women Who Opened the West" while another is "The Women Who Civilized the West." The Harvey Girls—because their story parallels that of the western railroad—exhibited a willingness to relocate to an unknown "Wild West" in search of employment. That characteristic set them apart from the sisterhood who remained behind in the East or Midwest for a more secure life. The Harvey Girls often became the "founding mothers of entire towns" after they left Harvey's service. They were neither political activists nor spinsters, because many did find romance and stable marriages. "They were most often ordinary women who valued themselves and believed they had something to offer [with] enough self-motivation to leave home and loved ones in pursuit of ... money, a chance to travel, a home away from mother and father, or even a husband." One writer observes that "they... kept the West supplied with food and wives." The Harvey Girls served from the 1880s until the World War II years. *Harvey Houses of New Mexico: Historic Hospitality from Raton to Deming. The Harvey Girls: Women Who Civilized the West. The Harvey Girls: Women Who Opened the West.*

Harwood, Emily Jane. He to preach, she to teach. Emily Harwood came to New Mexico soon after cessation of the Civil War with her Methodist minister husband Dr. Thomas Harwood —he to preach, she to teach. Their talents and abilities complemented each other. As his helpmate, they later established what was to become the Harwood School and Home for Girls in Albuquerque. It was followed in 1893 by their Boys' Biblical and Industrial School. Theirs were among the first nondenominational public schools in New Mexico. (1842–1902). *Notable New Mexico Women. Women in Education: New Mexico.*

Tura A. Hawk, Courtesy of Special Collections and University Archives, Iowa State University.

Hawk, Tura A. Home extension leader/suffrage advocate. A transplanted Midwesterner, Tura Hawk, a suffrage advocate, arrived in New Mexico around 1916 to become the state coordinator of home demonstration agents. Those intrepid women taught needed hands-on skills with rural homemakers in the home, the farm, and the community. Hawk was reputed to be Iowa's first home demonstration agent. She is said to have created a sensation when she took a blacksmithing course at Iowa State College. David V. Holtby writes that Hawk "immediately made her presence felt" in her new environment. Hawk enthusiastically supported Herbert Hoover's plan of "Winning the War [WWI] in the Kitchen" and organized large gatherings of women throughout New Mexico to promote meatless meals. (birth and death dates not available). *Lest We Forget: World War I and New Mexico.*

Head, Elen Agnes Kastner. Unyielding conservative newspaperwoman. In 1951 Agnes Head launched the *Hobbs Flare* newspaper which grew into an institution in her home base of Hobbs in deeply conservative southeastern New Mexico. Head had previously published the *Lovington Leader.* A staunch conservative, Head gained national attention for her practice of publishing the names and amounts received of all recipients of public welfare funds. She entered journalism as an investigative reporter. As a delegate to the 1969 state Constitutional Convention, Head was noted for her stand against ratification of a revised constitution. A community center in Hobbs is named for her. (1908–1992). *Notable New Mexico Women.* Find A Grave Memorial.

Henderson, Alice Corbin. Leading light of the Santa Fe literati. Alice Corbin Henderson, a Chicago poet and journal editor, fled the Midwest in 1916 with her distinguished artist husband William Penhallow Henderson and their daughter to Santa Fe, seeking a cure for her tuberculosis. In Chicago, she had known Carl Sandburg, Ezra Pound, Vachel Lindsay, Edgar Lee Masters, and Witter Bynner. Bynner was soon also to make his home in the "City Different." In Santa Fe, her circle of friends included Mary Austin, Willa Cather, D.H. Lawrence, and Witter Bynner. Soon Henderson was actively involved in the Santa Fe literary scene, inviting Bynner, Sandburg, and others to give readings. The result was her anthology of verse about her new homeland entitled *The Turquoise Trail* published in 1928. Another of her books of poetry about New Mexico is *Red Earth: Poems of New Mexico*. Critics consider *Brothers of Light: The Penitentes of the Southwest* to be perhaps the most important of her work. Henderson's husband, who shared his wife's fascination with New Mexico's Indian and Spanish heritage, illustrated that book for her. (1881–1949). *Santa Fe and Taos: The Writer's Era.* Notable New Mexico Women.

Henderson, Eva Pendleton. Penned coming-of-age memoir of southern New Mexico. Eva Henderson is the author of *Wild Horses: A Turn-Of-The-Century Prairie Girlhood* and *Wild Horses in My Blood: An 1890s Girlhood in New Mexico.* Accounts say Henderson was a member of the historic western ranching Chisum family. A frontier school teacher at age sixteen, Henderson's philosophy can be expressed simply: "Life is nothing but a coming and a going." Her life was not always easy, and she reflected that in these words: "Beauty lasts, peace does not." (1890–1986). *Wild Horses: A Turn-of-the-Century Prairie Girlhood. Wild Horses in My Blood: An 1890s Girlhood in New Mexico.*

Hestia, Mary. FDR's pottery "Poster Girl." Mary Hestia, also known as "Acoma Mary," was one of the first Native American potters to see the advantages of marketing Pueblo pottery to railroad passengers traveling through New Mexico. New Mexico historian and author Don Bullis has written that she is recognized as the finest Acoma Pueblo potter of the early twentieth century. Hestia traveled often to Washington and became popular as an unofficial potter to President Franklin D. Roosevelt. Her work soon decorated many government offices. Hestia deserves to be classed as a Modernist. (1881–1980). http://www.adobegallery.com/artist/Mary_Histia_1881_1973688.

Hicks, Pearl H. Foster. Albuquerque civil rights activist, early real estate broker. Pearl Hicks and her husband began life in Albuquerque modestly: he as a worker for the Santa Fe Railway, she running a barbecue stand. With their savings, the couple's business activities morphed into real estate, buying and selling properties, and assisting prospective minority buyers with mortgages and financial advice. In the meantime, Pearl also made time to participate in civil rights activities on behalf of African Americans and to work for improved voting rights. Albuquerque's African American community is the richer for her work. (1898–1980). *History of Hope: The African American Experience in New Mexico.*

Hoffman, Dolores "Dody" Garcia. From clerk to director at Sandia National Laboratories. Dody Hoffman is retired director of the Sandia

National Laboratories and is in private business. Sandia National Laboratories is an engineering and science laboratory in Albuquerque operated for the US Department of Energy's National Nuclear Security Administration. Its mission is to provide engineering and science support for America's nuclear weapons stockpile. Growing up in Hispanic rural New Mexico, Dody Hoffman frequently heard from her parents "que no hay hada mas importante que la educación," (there is nothing more important than an education). She took the stricture to heart, earning a bachelor's and master's degree. "Each of us," she believes, "defines success for ourselves through a uniquely personal road map, but seldom do we travel the road to success alone." (birth date unavailable). *Mujeres Valerosas ... meet the extraordinary women of the New Mexico Hispanic Women's Council.*

Hornig, Lilli Schlenk. Manhattan Project scientist. Lilli Hornig, a native of Czechoslovakia, accompanied her husband to Los Alamos Laboratory during World War II where he had a post waiting for him. After being asked to try out for a secretarial position, Lilli's scientific skills were recognized, and she was given a job in a group working with plutonium chemistry. Later it was decided that plutonium chemistry was too dangerous for women, and so she worked on high-explosive lenses instead. While at Los Alamos, Llili was among a group of scientists who petitioned the government urging that the first atom bomb be detonated on an uninhabited island. After leaving New Mexico, Honig became a chemistry professor and activist in women in science. (1921–2017). *Boston Globe.*

Lilli Schlenk Hornig.
Los Alamos National Laboratory.

Hoppes, Alice Faye Kent. Courageous leader and fearless spokeswoman against racial injustice. Former New Mexico governor Bill Richardson called Alice Hoppes "a leader who worked tirelessly to draw attention to the needs of New Mexico's African-American community." Hoppes was president of the Albuquerque NAACP for twelve years. "Alice came of age at a very important time in this country ... a time of Martin Luther King Jr.," said former Albuquerque mayor Martin Chávez. "And she believed very much in that dream and never deviated from [it]... New Mexico used to call itself a tri-cultural state, with Anglos, Hispanics and Indians, but things changed when Hoppes came along to point out it's a multi-cultural state that includes blacks," said Chávez. Born in Tucumcari, Hoppes was the only Black student in her school. Hoppes recalled how, as a child, she bristled at being excluded from the public swimming pool, being sent into the balcony at the movie theater, and hearing a teacher tell racial jokes in high school. She said that, after listening to the teacher use the word "nigger," Hoppes raised her hand and asked him to stop. She was suspended. But, Hoppes said, the teacher never again used the slur in her presence. Hoppes once told lawmakers, "Only by illuminating the history of African-Americans can we eradicate the myths and distortions responsible for problems in communications that still exist." (1921–2017). *Albuquerque Journal,* October 2, 2003.

Hospers, Hendrina. Missionary to the Jicarilla. Hendrina Hospers was a missionary of the Women's Board of Domestic Missions of the Reformed Church in Oklahoma to the Mescalero and Jicarilla Apaches in New Mexico. Hospers began work with the Jicarilla in 1914 following their release from captivity the previous year, and remained with them until her retirement in 1946. She grew up in a Dutch-American Protestant colony in Iowa that was led by her father. The colony was built around church and school, and Hendrina participated in both. (1880–1968). "Are You White or Dutch?" Hendrina hospers...wwwcommons.nwciowa.edu/northwesternreview/vol4/iss1/2/.

Howells, The. Santa Fe activists and philanthropists. Lifelong friends Eleanor Brownell and Alice Howland combined their last names, some say for convenience's sake. They had owned a girls' school in Pennsylvania before retiring to Santa Fe in 1941. They commissioned prominent architect John

Gaw Meem to design their eleven-room home and soon became pivotal philanthropic figures in Santa Fe. They played key roles in the Santa Fe branch of the English-Speaking Union and the Society of Friends, operated a preparatory school at Bishop's Lodge, and were members of the League of Women Voters. The two helped establish the Santa Fe Opera in 1957 with Eleanor as its first president and entertained composer Igor Stravinsky. They also established an endowment for the Santa Fe Public Library. Alice Howland (1883–1964). No birth or death dates for Eleanor Brownell.

Dorothy B. Hughes.

Hughes, Dorothy B. Crime fiction writer, critic, historian. Dorothy Hughes studied at Columbia University and won an award from the Yale Series of Younger Poets for her first book of poetry, *Dark Certainty* (1931). In 1939 she wrote *Pueblo on the Mesa: The First Fifty Years of the University of New Mexico*. After unsuccessful manuscripts, she published *The So Blue Marble* in 1940. A New York-based mystery, it won praise for its hardboiled prose, which was due in part to Hughes's editor, who demanded she cut 25,000 words. Hughes published thirteen more novels, the best known of which are *In a Lonely Place* (1947) and *Ride the Pink Horse* (1946).

Both were made into successful films. In the early fifties, Hughes largely stopped writing fiction, preferring to focus on criticism, for which she won an Edgar Award. In 1978, the Mystery Writers of America presented her with the Grand Master Award for literary achievement. Over the course of her career, she wrote fourteen novels, the majority of which were published between 1940 and 1952. (1904–1993).

Hurd, Henriette Wyeth, "Bini." Key figure in American painting dynasty. Henriette "Bini" Hurd was the daughter of famed illustrator N.C. Wyeth and the wife of equally famed painter Peter Hurd. She became "truly a woman of the American West" when she followed Peter to their Sentinel Ranch at Rincon near Ruidoso, New Mexico. Judy Alter writes in *Extraordinary Women of the American West* that Henriette Wyeth Hurd is considered "one of the great women painters of the twentieth century." Although she had no formal instruction, Henriette's real painting teacher was her father. He opposed her marriage to Hurd because he feared it would interfere with her painting. Alter writes that that never happened. There were other reasons Henriette gave up painting. She believed that a woman "should read to her children, forget slim hips, and be happy. The more a woman gives to people and the busier she is, the happier she is." Henriette always knew art was her destiny. "We all drew, and I was quite certain I would be splendid." Lyndon Johnson disliked the portrait Peter Hurd did of him, and likewise Richard Nixon disliked the painting Henriette did of his wife. Pat Nixon asked Henriette to change her expression in the painting but the artist refused. (1907–1997).

Henriette Wyeth Hurd.
Courtesy of Hurd La Rinconada Galley, Guest Homes & Sentinel Ranch Winery.

Indian Detour Couriers.

Indian Detour Couriers. Faces behind the Fred Harvey tours. The Couriers were staffed by elegant and sophisticated college-educated young women who, in the 1920s and 1930s, introduced American and international tourists to the Southwest and to all the beauty and wonder the area had to offer. The young women, an upscale version and counterpart to the Harvey Girls with a deep understanding of the Southwest and many with a command of the languages spoken there, were the daughters of important New Mexicans, including, for example, Claire Bursum, daughter of US Senator Holm O. Bursum. They were organized and trained by the venerable entrepreneur and author Erna Fergusson of Albuquerque. One Courier, a native German, was assigned to interpret and guide famed physicist Albert Einstein on his visit to the Grand Canyon and the Petrified Forest. Even celebrities such as famed author Willa Cather were not immune to the tour's demands for schedule-keeping. She writes, "but the Indian Detourists abound and the motor horn is the worm that dieth not." The Detours came into being in 1925 under the leadership of former British Army officer Major R. Hunter Clarkston. But his profligate spending, among other things, led to the company's ultimate demise. The lean years of 1933–1941 spelled the beginning of the end, but as as one observer puts it, "The amazing thing was not that the Indian Detours died, but that they didn't die sooner." She noted that "Depression, a war, mismanagement, private motoring, all should have sounded the death knell long before the 1960s (when it finally did)." The tours began in 1926 and died out in the 1960s. *The Southwestern Indian Detours: The story of the Fred Harvey/Santa Fe Railway Experiment in Detourism. The Selected Letters of Willa Cather.*

Irving-Gibbs, Fannye. Historian, civil rights activist. Fannye Irving-Gibbs was an expert on Black cowboys and the Buffalo Soldiers, US Cavalry troops so named for their hair and fierce fighting skills by the Native people of the American West. Irving-Gibbs never stopped learning and working, especially if it meant bringing about positive change for minorities. "She never stopped being involved, working with people and fighting for civil rights," said one co-worker. Irving-Gibbs dedicated herself to building awareness of the historical contributions made by Blacks in the West and getting scholars to reconsider how they viewed Black history. She published several books for public schools that included often-neglected Black history, including the first Spanish Blacks who stopped in the Albuquerque area during the late 1500s and early 1600s as settlers on their way to Santa Fe. Irving-Gibbs fought for equity in housing, advocating for youths and education while furthering her own education. Irving-Gibbs, who was Rio Rancho's first court clerk, was seventy-seven when she earned her master's degree from the University of New Mexico. (1914–2006). *Albuquerque Journal*, October 27, 2006.

Jackson, Ida O. Pioneer Black educator. Clovis schools were segregated when Ida O. Jackson arrived from Texas in 1926 to teach African -American youth. Starting with two students in Bethlehem Baptist Church, she encouraged early education and by 1935 was teaching thirty-five students in a one-room schoolhouse. The school was named Lincoln Jackson School to honor her and the nation's 16th president. Enrollment topped one hundred by the 1940s with high school training offered as well. Ida also taught Sunday school, opened her home to those needing housing, and launched the Federated Progressive Club for Black Women, working for community improvement. One resident recalled that Jackson "took in strays and people without housing." Although those tenants promised to pay, most did not. (1891–1961). New Mexico Historic Women Marker Initiative. *History of Hope: The African American Experience in New Mexico. Bridges: New Mexico Black Women, 1900–1950.*

James, Rebecca Salsbury. Encouraged colcha embroidery revival. Rebecca Salsbury James was born in London to Buffalo Bill's Wild West Show business manager and opera singer Rachel Samuels. James came to Taos with Georgia O'Keeffe in 1928. She soon found herself caught up in the Spanish colonial folk art of colcha embroidery and encouraged others to take it up as well. She began creating miniature "needle paintings" and exhibited throughout the country. The *Albuquerque Journal* writes that Salsbury was an important component of a "dysfunctional quartet of artists and lovers [who] had a lasting impact on modernism." Salsbury was the least-known but nonetheless "formed the warp to their weaving." Salsbury's future husband was Paul Strand. Salsbury figured prominently in O'Keeffe's life, observes the biography *Foursome* by Carolyn Burke. James taught O'Keeffe to drive, an important survival skill on those rough roads of northern New Mexico. Salsbury divorced Strand, then married an operator of a Taos trading post. "She became known for her glass paintings as well as for an ability to drink men under the table." (1885–1939). *Albuquerque Journal*, June 9, 2019. Kathleen Roberts. *Notable New Mexico Women.*

Jaramillo, Cleofas Martinez. Author and fierce protector of New Mexico culture. Cleofas Jaramillo wrote *Romance of a Little Village Girl*—her autobiography and memoir and sequel to *Shadows of the Past*—and the cookbook *New Mexico Tasty Recipes*. She accomplished this despite decrying a lack of English skills. Jaramillo grew up in a privileged life of genteel Spanish society in late nineteenth century northern New Mexico. She was the archetypical village girl. Nonetheless, she later displayed strength and resilience in the face of tragedy: the death of two infant children, of her young husband, the ensuing muddle of his financial affairs, and the shocking murder of her teenaged daughter. She called her husband's death the breaking of the "cord of life." Jaramillo was active in preserving the New Mexico Hispanic culture through founding the Sociedad Folklórico. Her writing reflected this interest. *Shadows of the Past* (*Sombras del Pasado*) was one such attempt because, as she explained, "I have watched with regret the passing of old Spanish customs and the rapid adoption of modern Anglo customs..." (1878–1956). *Romance of a Little Village Girl.*

Jaramillo, Debbie. Santa Fe's first woman mayor outspoken for her people. The *Los Angeles Times* called Debbie Jaramillo "independent and fiercely protective" of Santa Fe's vanishing Hispanic culture and traditions. Jaramillo, elected on a pledge to reverse trends that had transformed her home town into a haven for rich tourists and transplants with little or no regard for the effect on average-income residents, viewed herself as a "Chicana infiltrator." In 1998 she campaigned on the slogan "Take back Santa Fe." She opposed gentrification of Santa Fe, which pushed the primarily Hispanic local population out of its historical neighborhoods. "We painted our downtown brown and moved the brown people out," she declared. Jaramillo believed Santa Fe's ethnic heritage was packaged and sold as "Santa Fe-style" in upscale galleries, boutiques, and restaurants sprouting up in former Hispanic areas as average residents were forced out. Jaramillo wanted to help those who had been long neglected: "They happen to be mostly Hispanic." She was defeated for re-election after one term marked by controversy. (1952–). *Los Angeles Times,* December 12, 1994. Wikipedia.

Jaramillo, Mari-Luci, PhD. First Mexican-American woman ambassador. Mari-Luci Jaramillo exemplified the best of the New Mexico values of hard work and love of education. While attending school, Jaramillo worked in her father's shop shining shoes. Later, she cleaned houses and waited tables to help pay her way to New Mexico Highlands University in Las Vegas. After graduation, she became an elementary school teacher. Later, Jaramillo joined the faculty at the University of New Mexico and served as associate dean, vice president, and assistant to the president. In 1976, she was appointed ambassador of the United States to Honduras, becoming the first Mexican-American woman to be a US representative to another country. Her career always focused on helping children and families in poverty through education, policy, leadership, and diplomacy. She wrote two books about her life: *Madame Ambassador: The Shoemaker's Daughter* and *Sacred Seeds: A Girl, Her Abuelos,* as well as the *Heart of Northern New*

Mexico with Cecilla Navarrete. (1928–2019). https://news./unm/edu/a/ distinguished-career-in-education.

Jenkins, Myra Ellen, PhD. Keeping busy never a problem. Myra Ellen Jenkins could have provided the slogan for many of the women in this book when she said, "I don't have a problem with keeping interested. I have so many doggone interests I can't keep up with them." *Women in Education: New Mexico* captured her essence by calling her "a prodigious author and researcher." She did indeed know New Mexico. "Dr. J." joined the newly created New Mexico State Records Center and Archives in 1953 and was state historian from 1967 until 1980. Her emphasis was land grants, water rights, and Pueblo Indian research. Jenkins played a pivotal role in developing New Mexico's modern historic preservation movement. She was a founding member of the Cultural Properties Review Committee—the body that approves historic markers. She helped develop many of the laws and policies New Mexico uses to preserve its past. Jenkins assisted pueblos and tribes in retaining their ancestral lands. In the 1970s she intervened to prevent the transfer of land grant records to federal repositories, thus retaining a vital component of New Mexico history. She co-authored *A Brief History of New Mexico*, considered the essential guide to New Mexico history for the state's schoolchildren. (1916–1993). New Mexico Historic Women Marker Initiative. *Buried Treasures: Famous and Unusual Gravesites in New Mexico History.*

Jette, Eleanor B. Manhattan Project insider. Eleanor Jette was the wife of key New Mexico project leader Eric Jette who helped develop the atomic bomb on the highly secret Manhattan Project at Los Alamos during World War II. She used that position and insight to write the intriguing story of "the City on the Hill." Jette said her book *Inside Box 1663* shone a light on "the lives of men and women who lived and worked in grim secrecy to hasten the end of the war." Jette added that her book focused on the lives of men and women who lived and worked to hasten the end of the war. "The book is the story of censored mail, and sharing a post office box with every other person in town PO Box 1663, Santa Fe, NM." (1907–1963). *Inside Box 1663. Buried Treasures: Famous and Unusual Gravesites in New Mexico History.*

Jones, Ruth Bush. PR practitioner extraordinaire. A public relations specialist with the US Forest Service in New Mexico, Ruth Jones often attended meetings of the Albuquerque chapter of the Public Relations Society of America wearing her trademark Smokey the Bear cap. She frequently would be the only woman in a room of ten men or more. Jones paved the way for a dramatic expansion in the number of women in the practice of public relations in New Mexico. While working for the University of New Mexico, she is credited with three PR "firsts" in New Mexico: getting publicity placed in a newspaper, securing photo usage in a newspaper, and securing publication of a feature picture in a newspaper. (1903–1987). *Hobbs Flare.* David Smoker, Ron Hamm.

Eunice Gronvold Kalloch.
Courtesy of Elwyn B. Robinson Department of Special Collections, Chester Fritz Library, University of North Dakota.

Kalloch, Eunice Gronvold. Health and environmental activist, author. Eunice Gronvold Kalloch was born in North Dakota, educated in the Upper Midwest, and earned a master's degree in geography before working in US Army intelligence at the Pentagon. Following marriage and the conclusion of World War II, she moved to Albuquerque and became active in many community and civic organizations. Governor Bruce King declared a Eunice Kalloch Day in her honor and an Albuquerque park was named after her. She wrote *First Ladies of New Mexico* with Ruth K. Hall (1982). Kalloch also wrote of her parents in *Mama and Papa Were Pioneers*. (1908–1988). Eunice Gronvold Papers, 1873–1983. University of North Dakota Department of Special Collections. Eunice Kalloch Papers, 1948–1980. University of New Mexico Center for Southwest Research and Special Collections.

Keleher, Julia. Teacher, author. Julia Keleher was a sister of famed New Mexico lawyer and author Will Keleher. She taught literature and creative writing for thirty years at the University of New Mexico. An award is given annually at the University of New Mexico to a teacher who demonstrates a strong commitment to teaching. Keleher was a regular contributor to *New Mexico Quarterly Review* for many years and edited *New Mexico Folklore Magazine.* (1894–1980). Notable New Mexico Women.

Margaret Judith Kennedy.
Thomas C. Donnelly Library, Highlands University.

Kennedy, Margaret Judith. Early figure in New Mexico education. Margaret Kennedy taught in the Roswell, New Mexico, schools before joining the faculty of New Mexico Normal University (now Highlands University) in 1915. She was dean of women, president of the New Mexico Education Association and one of the first women members of the New Mexico Board of Education. Esteemed by students and colleagues alike, she epitomized the teacher and the woman of her day. One of her favorite expressions was: "Sweet is the voice of a low-voiced woman but exceedingly exasperating when she cannot be heard." (1879–1964). *Notable New Mexico Women. Women in Education: New Mexico.*

Alice M. King.

King, Alice M. Imparted new meaning to the term "First Lady." Alice King was "First Lady" of New Mexico three times during her husband Bruce's three non-consecurive terms as governor of New Mexico from 1971–1975, 1979–1983, and again from 1991–1995. As such, his wife, Alice, used her time as "First Lady" to actively advance the many causes dear to her heart and those for the benefit of the state's citizens, particularly children. She was especially devoted to education. During her lifetime she was associated with some thirty-five organizations, most frequently as chairman. *The First Ladies of New Mexico* called her "the state's number one volunteer," adding that she gave her position "a new dimension." (1930–2008). *The First Ladies of New Mexico*.

Kinyon, Annette Ford. Silver City suffragist. During the early 1910s, Annette Kinyon was the most active suffragist in Silver City. Annette and her husband had moved from the East to Silver City, where she organized the first kindergarten school at the local teachers' college. Annette soon shifted her attention to the Silver City Woman's Club, part of the enormous General Federation of Women's Clubs. Club minutes track Annette's growing interest in feminist politics. In May 1913, she was elected president. Elizabeth Warren and Isabel Eckles —the two most prominent women in Silver City of the time—joined the club as Kinyon rose to leadership. They too were suffragists. At a time when the national suffrage groups paid little attention to New Mexico, women's clubs spearheaded voting rights. The state conference of women's clubs in Silver City in 1914 was the major event of Kinyon's two-year presidency. Delegates adopted resolutions urging statewide suffrage and equal property rights. The meeting was a triumph for Kinyon. She was elected first vice-president of the state federation. Her club, the New Mexico Federation, and the GFWC were declared supporters of suffrage. Other interests soon collided with the realities of World War I. The Silver City club suspended activities for the duration of the war, and Kinyon threw herself into volunteer work, especially for the Red Cross and successive campaigns for the Liberty Loans. Later, the National American Woman Suffrage Association and the National Woman's Party helped push the state into ratifying suffrage in February 1920, the thirty-second of the necessary thirty-six states required by law to do so. (1872–1935). "Annette Kinyon," 2019. Stephen Fox.

Klapp, Mary Ellen Hall Warren, "Mollie." Homesteader. Eighty million acres of public land in the West went into private ownership by 1900 through the Homestead Act. New Mexico drew hundreds of settlers who built homes and farmed one hundred sixty-acre allotments in pursuit of a better life. Mollie Klapp was one such person. Born in Illinois, by 1900 she was widowed in Oklahoma with seven children when she decided to move to Moriarty, New Mexico—"pinto bean capital of the world." The Estancia Valley is well-suited to dryland farming and helped New Mexico become the nation's fourth largest pinto-bean producer by 1916 when more than two million pounds were harvested. Mollie farmed, taught school, and remarried. Her hard life led to institutionalization at the state mental health hospital in Las Vegas where she worked as a seamstress and housekeeper, dying from "exhaustion." (1862–1933). New Mexico Historic Scenic Markers.

Lily Casey Klassner.

Klassner, Lily Casey. New Mexico frontier schoolmarm. Lily Casey Klassner's compelling story as a New Mexico frontier school teacher is related by Eve Ball in *My Girlhood Among Outlaws* and encapsulated in *Women in Education: New Mexico.* Lily's experience with the rough-and-ready classroom and everythin144g that went with it before New Mexico's school law1s were enacted was right out of a Hollywood movie script. Families in remote areas started a school when enough people who desired education and were willing to pay for it gathered together, says *Women in Education.* When Lily Casey (later Klassner) passed through present-day Mayhill in southern New Mexico, she was asked to teach. Thus, her career in education was launched. Area ranchers took up a subscription and came up with enough money to pay Lily $50 a month for six months. One of the rancher's wives was paid $10 a month for Lily's board and room with the understanding that Lily would pitch in with morning and evening chores. A schoolhouse went up, and students ranging in age from six to nineteen came. After a year, Lily left and met and married Joe Klassner. After her divorce a few years later, she enrolled at New Mexico Normal College (now Highlands University) in Las Vegas and qualified for teaching. She entered the classroom in the Lincoln County schools as a newly minted teacher, relying on her Spanish language skills to work with bilingual students. (1862–1946). *Women in Education: New Mexico. My Girlhood Among Outlaws.*

Klauber, Alice. Discovered herself in New Mexico. The daughter of a wealthy San Diego, California, merchant, Alice Klauber gravitated toward the arts, eventually becoming San Diego's first lady of the arts. Klauber later was to have a similar influence on the arts in Santa Fe. As a noted painter with important connections to the art world, it was natural that she should be asked to chair the Fine Arts Department of the Panama Pacific Exposition in San Diego in 1915. However, it was in New Mexico where Klauber found herself. As Leslie Poling-Kempes writes in *Ladies of the Canyons*, Klauber discovered her "Santa Fe self which is a new woman." She was a devoted friend of Natalie Curtis, and though Santa Fe wasn't her primary residence, she was intimately involved with the modern artists who came there in support of the Museum of Art (now the New Mexico Museum of Art), which opened in 1917. (1871–1951). *Ladies of the Canyons*. Jennifer Levin, *Pasotiempo*, November 27, 2015

Kleven, Concha de Ortiz y Pino. Grande Dame of New Mexico. Born into a prominent New Mexico political family two years before statehood, Concha de Ortiz y Pino Kleven was educated at the Loretto Academy in Santa Fe. Her upbringing was the foundation of all she achieved, ranging from official and volunteer posts at the local and national level in civic, religious, and cultural arenas. Biographer Kathryn Cordova quotes her as saying, "Life is so interesting, if you don't sit on it. The worst thing...is the accumulation of goods that don't help anyone. It's stinginess of the heart." An example of her philosophy: she founded the state's first vocational school in her home village of Galisteo and taught traditional New Mexico arts and crafts. She served three terms in the New Mexico Legislature. At age thirty, Kleven became the Democratic majority whip, the first

Concha de Ortiz y Pino Kleven

woman to hold such a position in state government. Among her causes were allowing women to serve on juries, equalizing financing for urban and rural schools, and establishing mandatory middle school Spanish-language instruction. Kleven also spearheaded education and rehabilitation for prisoners in the state penitentiary. (1910–2006). Associated Press. Santa Fe Living Treasures. New Mexico Historic Women Marker Initiative. *Notable New Mexico Women. Women in Education: New Mexico.*

Klinekole, Virginia. Native American leader. Virginia Klinekole was the first woman in the United States to gain leadership of a major American Indian tribe. In 1959, Klinekole ousted longtime tribal power Wendell Chino for leadership of the Mescalero Apache tribe near Ruidoso. Her accomplishments were many. Klinekole established a loan program for Mescalero Apaches and led her government in purchasing homes for tribal members living on Mescalero land. She pushed economic development. "She served the tribe during an exciting time in the tribe's history," said a successor, Mark Chino. Klinekole stressed the importance of education for her people. She served as a member of the Tularosa school board and was a member of the Mescalero school board. Klinekole kept tabs on children who missed school and visited their parents to encourage attendance. Klinekole also helped tribal members in developing an Apache language dictionary. (1924–2011). *Albuquerque Journal.* Rene Romo. March 24, 2011.

Gene Kloss.

Kloss, Alice (Gene) Geneva Glasier. Artist, print maker. Gene Kloss is nationally known for her prints of the New Mexico landscape and of the ceremonies of the Pueblo people, all executed from memory. Her name is synonymous with copperplate etching. She has been called "one of the great printmakers" in the state's history." She was the first woman inducted as a print maker into the National Academy of Design. *Art News* has called her "one of our most sensitive and sympathetic interpreters of the Southwest." *Albuquerque Journal* arts writer Kathaleen Roberts has cited Kloss's compositions of light and dark with "coalescing into mythical New Mexico landscapes." Kloss came to Taos in the 1920s with poet husband

Phillips Kloss where she found a mostly male-dominated cadre of artists. Kloss was not intimidated. She decried the term "woman artist," once remarking that "I say I'm a woman, and an artist. But I'm not a woman artist. I wouldn't ... [call myself] a woman lawyer or a woman teacher, or a woman musician." Early working conditions were primitive. Her first etching press, a sixty-pound machine, was installed at their camp in Taos Canyon by cementing it to a large rock. That was eventually replaced by a mammoth 1,084 pound Sturges etching press purchased from a defunct greeting card company. From her spare life on the eastern edge of Taos with neither water nor electricity, but plenty of firewood, kerosene and inspiration, Gene Kloss informed the art world of the special beauty inherent in American Southwestern images: the churches, the Native American faces, the mountains and valleys, the dances, and intricate rhythms of life in a part of the United States that remains essentially unchanged. With the years and the continual dedication came honors, both national and international. The Smithsonian, the National Gallery, The Corcoran Gallery of Fine Art, the Library of Congress, and the Metropolitan Museum of Art all house the works of Gene Kloss in their permanent collections. (1903–1996). *Art News, Albuquerque Journal,* October 25, 2018.

Matilda R. Wright Koehler. Courtesy of Silver City NM Museum.

Koehler, Matilda R. Wright. From school principal to sidewalk superintendent. Matilda Koehler supervised Elizabeth Warren's work crew constructing downtown Silver City sidewalks, among other projects, after leaving a career in public education in Silver City. Many miles of sidewalks later, the two engaged in a full-scale general contracting business, constructing and remodeling homes and businesses, and tackling public works projects. Koehler (who signed her name M. R. Koehler) originally came West in 1888 to help organize the

New Mexico A&M College in Las Cruces where she became New Mexico's first woman college teacher along with Anna Hadley. Koehler served fifteen years with the Silver City schools and was regarded as one of the best educators the community had ever known. She conceded, however, that construction was the preferable job "because it paid better." (1861–1946). "Coloring Outside the Lines: Empowered Women in Territorial and Early-Statehood Silver City" *Desert Exposure*. March 2012. *Women in Education: New Mexico*.

Kohn, Yetta Goldsmith. Bavarian born, New Mexico success. Born in Bavaria and widowed in New Mexico, Yetta Goldsmith Kohn made a lasting impression on her homeland in many ways. Her family arrived in the United States in 1853, settling in Kansas. When she was seventeen, she married Samuel Kohn, a merchant. The couple had six children. The Kohns moved several times in search of opportunity. In 1868, they left Kansas for the second time and moved to Las Vegas, New Mexico. When they arrived, Samuel opened a store and Yetta worked as a seamstress. Yetta was just thirty-six when Samuel died in 1878. She and her son Howard continued to run the thriving hide and wool shop. She was an astute businesswoman, a rancher who loved the land, and a philanthropist. Yetta ran the family store and raised her family alone. She later moved to La Cinta on the Canadian River where she opened another store, became the postmistress, started a bank, and operated a ferry. By 1907, the family businesses were prospering. Eight years later, tragedy struck when son Charles died on his honeymoon. While the family awaited the return of Charles's body, another son George, died of a heart attack. Never having fully recovered from those tragedies, Yetta died fifteen months later at seventy-four. (1843–1917). New Mexico Historic Women Marker Initiative. Find A Grave Memorial.

Yetta Goldsmith Kohn. Find A Grave Memorial.

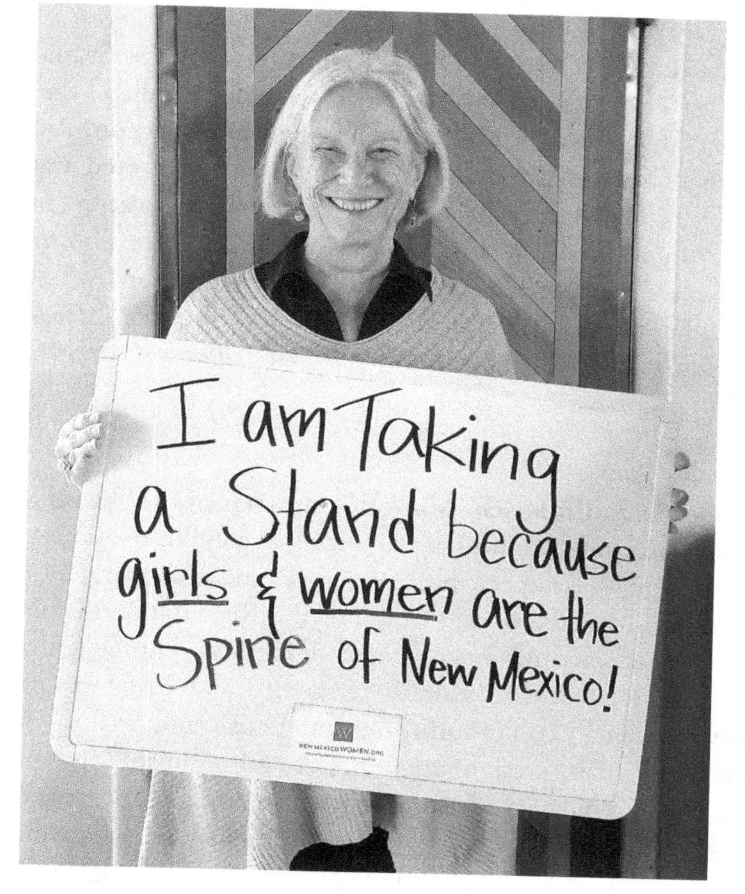

Ruth L. Kovnat.

Kovnat, Ruth L. Broke the legal education roadblocks. When Ruth Kovnat became a tenure- track professor at the Temple University School of Law in 1971, she was its first female law professor and among the first female law professors in the nation. Four years later, she joined the faculty at the University of New Mexico School of Law. Although her emphasis is environmental, constitutional law and federal jurisdiction, Kovnat has studied and taught a wide range of legal topics and contributes to those fields. She is on the board of directors of the New Mexico Center on Law and Poverty and is a past member of the New Mexico Water Quality Control Commission. She also studied water quality issues in Albuquerque's South Valley. Kovnat received the Governor's Award for Outstanding New Mexico Women. (1939-) lawschool.unm.edu/faculty/kovnat/index.html

Kramer, Dorothy Dunn. Shepherded the "Golden Age" of Native American Painting. Dorothy Dunn Kramer created the Studio School at the Santa Fe Indian School in what some have called "the Golden Age" of Indian painting under her tutelage and inspiration. Among the accomplished Native American artists whom she mentored was Pablita Velarde. In 1954, Kramer was awarded the French government's *Ordre des Palmes academiques*. Kramer wrote *American Indian Painting of the Southwest and Plains Area*. Noted Santa Fe artist and muralist Olive Rush was among her many advocates. (1903–1992). *Olive Rush: A Hoosier Artist in New Mexico. Buried Treasures: Famous and Unusual Gravesites in New Mexico History.*

Kurath, Gertrude Prokosch. Musical interpreter of the Tewas. Daughter of a pianist, Gertrude Kurath began dancing as a child. In addition to that interest, she was a researcher, prolific author, and ethnomusicologist. She first experienced the dance and music of the Rio Grande Pueblos in her fifties and co-authored *Music and Dance of the Tewa Pueblos* with Antonio Garcia of San Juan Pueblo. Kurath researched and wrote extensively on the study of dance, co-authoring several books and writing hundreds of articles. Her main areas of interest were ethnomusicology and dance ethnology, with some of her best known works being "Panorama of Dance Ethnology" in *Current Anthropology*. She made substantial contributions to the study of Amerindian dance and to dance theory. From 1958 to January 1972 she was dance editor for the journal *Ethnomusicology*. (1903–1992). *Daughters of the Desert.* Wikipedia.

Ruth Barker Laughlin.

Laughlin, Ruth (Alexander, Ruth Barker Laughlin). Activist writer, suffragist. Born into a prominent New Mexico Territorial suffragist family, it was natural for that to be the career path Ruth Laughlin (she wrote under maiden name) would follow. With encouragement from her parents, Judge Napoleon Laughlin and her suffragist mother Katie Kimbrough Laughlin, Ruth studied journalism at Colorado College and Columbia University before working in archaeology in Guatemala, Mexico, and her home state. All along, she found time to be active in politics and the suffragist movement. Married twice with children, she spoke at a 1916 rally in Santa Fe along with national suffragist leaders Doris Stevens and Ella St. Clair. Later she became active in the League of Women Voters. Widely published, she wrote for *The New York Times* and the *Ladies Home Journal* on contemporary Southwestern political and social issues. Laughlin is the author of two books still considered Southwestern classics: *The Romance of Santa Fe and the Southwest*, an extensive history of her home town, and *The Wind Leaves No Shadow*. The latter is an historical novel of a young

Santa Fe 1830s woman struggling for respect and influence in a male-dominated society. (1889–1962). Erin Morse, Biographical Database of NAWSA Suffragists, University of New Mexico, and "50 Years Ago," *Santa Fe New Mexican,* November 2, 1962.

Leach, Frances. A natural. Frances Leach's exemplary mining career is told through contemporaneous newspaper accounts relating her discoveries. "Old times are recalled by the discovery last week of rich gold-bearing ore...south of the Burro Mountains and by a small stampede of miners to the new camp.... Credit for discovering the gold is given to Mrs. Leach, wife of the chief chemist of the Phelps Dodge Corporation at Tyrone." Born in West Virginia, Frances married Leach, an engineering graduate of Columbia University. Thereafter they began a colorful career in Mexico. Following the assassination in 1914 of President Francisco Madero and an ensuing revolution, they fled for New Mexico. Leach with her husband began visiting claims to investigate the possibility of fluorspar. She suspected the presence of gold and recovered samples...[upon] being assayed to be much richer than she had suspected. "That the rarest and most valuable of all minerals–radium–is to be found in Grant county has been proven beyond the shadow of a doubt... The credit for this remarkable and epoch-making discovery goes to a woman.... Mrs. Leach holds no university degree in geology or mineralogy but her husband is [a] geologist....and close association with him...developed in her a wonderful natural bent along these lines. It was Mrs. Leach's trained eye, aided by her woman's intuition that sensed something unusual in the ore which lay scattered on the dump.... [of a prospect]. She asked her husband what it was. He did not know and a test was decided upon. It did not take long to establish... that they had something unusual but it took many lengthy and elaborate tests–all the best kind of fun for the Leaches–to discover just what it was. Once on the trail of a rare mineral nothing could stop these two ardent scientists and finally, they decided that they had torbernite. It was a copper phosphate known previously to exist only in Portugal. Many rare minerals are valueless but this one as a source of radium is exceedingly valuable..." (1882–1958). *Silver City Enterprise,* May 30 1919, March 12, 1920, and January 1, 1959.

Lee, Frances Marron. Educator, rancher, political activist. Frances Lee and her husband Floyd operated one of the oldest ranches in New Mexico, near San Mateo. Being a ranch wife was only one aspect of the busy life of this teacher, chairman of the Grants Board of Education, a member of the Board of Regents of the University of New Mexico, and first president of the New Mexico Schools Study Council. Lee exerted her considerable political influence to inaugurate the school consolidation movement in New Mexico. Sixteen years later, every county in the state had adopted that pattern. A Republican National Committeewoman, Lee was appointed as permanent United States delegate to the Inter-American Commission on Women. (1902–1990). *Notable New Mexico Women.* Find A Grave Memorial. *New Mexico Women in Education: New Mexico.*

Manuelita "Mela" de Atocha Lucero Leger. *Albuquerque Journal.*

Leger, Manuelita "Mela" de Atocha Lucero." Bilingual education trailblazer. Although New Mexico's constitution protects Spanish-speaking students, school children were often punished for speaking Spanish. As an innovator in bilingual education, Mela Manuelita de Atocha Lucero Leger changed that by founding one of the nation's first bilingual multi-cultural schools—developing curricula, training teachers, and helping write the historic 1973 Bilingual Education Act. Mela's grandfather was blind, and at age four she enjoyed reading the newspapers to him in Spanish. After graduating from Loretto College in Denver, she and her husband raised seven children in Las Vegas, New Mexico. Mela received a Master's degree from Highlands University. She was one of a handful of educators to participate in the national debate and development of curriculum and tests for bilingual children. The fully bilingual, multi-cultural elementary school she started and ran was visited by policy makers and educators from Washington, DC, as well as other states. She also directed the Las Vegas Teacher Training Center. The center provided demonstration classes and in-service training in New Mexico bilingual education. (1928–2006). New Mexico Historic Women Marker Initiative.

Sister Mary DeSales Leheny.

Leheny, Mary DeSales MD, Sister. A member of the Order of Sisters of Charity, Sister Mary DeSales Leheny was missioned to St. Vincent's Hospital in Santa Fe in 1880 where she spent the rest of her religious and professional life. She worked first as a nurse-pharmacist, then in 1901 became a licensed physician. She is believed to be the first woman doctor in New Mexico Territory and one of the first in the country. In later years Sister Leheny was in charge of the St Vincent's Old Folks Home. (1856–1934). *Notable New Mexico Women*.

Lucy R. Lippard.

Lippard, Lucy R. Major literary figure, author, critic, curator. Lucy Lippard is an internationally known writer, art critic, activist, and curator. Among the first to recognize "dematerialization" in conceptual art, she was an early champion of feminist art. *The New York Times* has called her "a distinguished woman." Her *Undermining: A Wild Ride Through Land Use, Politics and Art in the Changing World* examines and criticizes the assault on public and Native American lands, especially New Mexico. Lippard excoriates tourism as a source of travel revenue grasped at by desperate economies. In New Mexico this means culture, "an acknowledged money-maker in the Land of Entrapment [sic]." Of this, a key component is archaeology with its focus on "dead Indians," as Lippard wryly casts it. "Native people are still considered by many to be another kind of natural resource...icons of the past rather than living citizens." Lippard also examines the impact of extraction industries upon Native American peoples, especially uranium mining upon the Navajo. She writes that, "We have been living in increasing porous borderlands, but after that black Tuesday (9/11), the previously insulated American world is different, full of holes previously only suspected, and an erosion of civil liberties hitherto considered sacrosanct." *Undermining and Down Country: The Tano of the Galiesto Basin, 1250–1782* serves as an inspiration to future generations. *Down Country* demonstrates Lippard's intellectual and emotional investment in her adopted homeland and examines those who peopled the Galiesto Basin for hundreds of years. Calling it "a community of communities" because of the relative proximity of its pueblos to each other, she underscores the importance of learning about them but warns that "There is always the danger of letting preoccupation with the past make us forget the future." (1937–). *The New York Times. Undermining: A Wild Ride Through Land Use, Politics, and Art in the Changing World. Down Country: The Tano of the Galisteo Basin. 1250–1782.* Telephone Interview with Ron Hamm.

Loftus, Lauretta. Broke the color barrier in Albuquerque schools. Although she had taught successfully for a decade in the Oklahoma public schools, Lauretta Loftus encountered a hostile attitude toward African Americans upon applying to the Albuquerque public schools (APS) in the late 1940s. She first sought a teaching post in 1949 but was turned away. She continued to apply while accepting employment with the Albuquerque Indian Health Service until she landed an interview with the APS superintendent. He told her he was hesitant to hire "colored" teachers because there had never been any in his system. Finally, in 1954, Loftus was hired as an elementary school teacher, thus becoming the first of her race to break the color barrier in New Mexico's largest school system. In addition to battling discrimination in the schools, Loftus participated in New Mexico sit-ins in the mid nineteen hundreds, especially at drugstores that barred Blacks from eating at their lunch counters. One publication observed that she "paved the way for others and inspired many." https:/en./wikipedia.org/wiki/pedia:meetup/women-of-new-mexico. *Noteworthy Black Women of New Mexico.*

Long, Emily G. Teaching exemplar. Much of Emily Long's teaching in New Mexico's coal camps in the 1930s and 1940s was of children of first-generation Italian, Greek, Spanish, Montenegrin, and Irish miners. She insisted that her unruly students stay at their desks until their work was completed. "With me," she told her mini-UN group of young scholars, "You are going to be very quiet, and work. If you don't, you'll miss supper at home tonight because you are going to stay in your seats until the work is done [even] if it takes all year." Needless to say, the threat did not need to be articulated very often. Emily often showed her compassionate side as well. She would return to the classroom a couple of hours after her young charges left at five in the afternoon to work with the children's parents to enable them to pass their citizenship examinations. (1885–1954). *Women in Education: New Mexico.*

Joan Potter Loveless and husband Oli Sihvonen.
Archives of North Carolina.

Loveless, Joan Potter. Weaver, author. Jean Potter Loveless wrote *Three Weavers*, a reminiscence of the lives and work of three Taos craftswomen covering forty years. Loveless came to Taos in the early 1950s fresh from college in North Carolina where she had studied weaving. When she and her artist husband and infant daughter arrived, they did not suspect that they would establish a relationship with the region that would pull them back again and again. In Taos, Loveless's life became intertwined with that of her friends Rachel Brown and Kristina Wilson. The women shared a love for the New Mexico landscape, their work as weavers and spinners, and the joys and sorrows of children and grandchildren. *The Three Weavers* relates the story of the evolution of their work—a relationship with wool unique to each weaver but for each intimately related to northern New Mexico. As their careers developed, the three participated in craft co-ops, educational programs, and commercial ventures. In her book, Loveless captures the spirit of Taos Valley, the texture of daily life, and the challenge of the creative process. (1928–2009). *The Three Weavers.*

Low Dog, Tieraona, MD.. Explorer of natural medicine. Dr. Tieraona Low Dog is a physician, author, and educator. Her exploration of natural medicine began more than thirty years ago with the study of midwifery, herbal medicine, massage therapy, and martial arts. She then went on to earn a medical degree from the University of New Mexico. Low Dog is passionate about empowering people with the knowledge needed for health and well-being. Birthdate not available. dr/lowdog.com/

Mabel Dodge Luhan

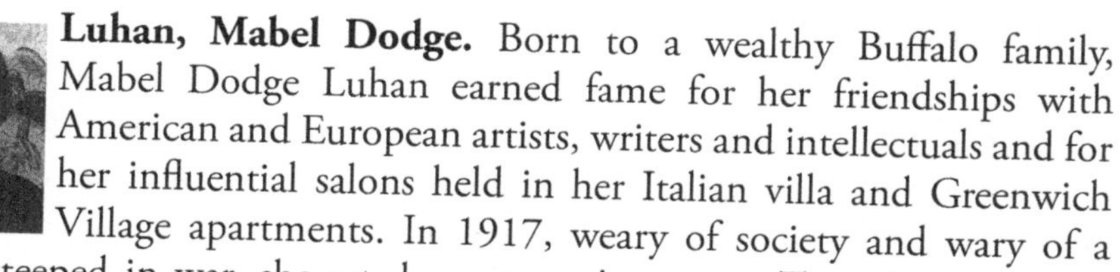

Luhan, Mabel Dodge. Born to a wealthy Buffalo family, Mabel Dodge Luhan earned fame for her friendships with American and European artists, writers and intellectuals and for her influential salons held in her Italian villa and Greenwich Village apartments. In 1917, weary of society and wary of a world steeped in war, she set down roots in remote Taos, New Mexico, then publicized the tiny town's inspirational beauty to the world, drawing a steady stream of significant guests to her adobe estate, including artists Georgia O'Keeffe and Dorothy Brett, poet Robinson Jeffers, and authors D. H. Lawrence and Willa Cather. Luhan could be difficult, complex and often cruel, yet she was also generous and supportive, establishing a solid reputation as a patron of the arts and as an author of widely read autobiographies, including *Winter in Taos, Lorenzo in Taos,* and the four-volume *Intimate Memories.* (1879–1962)

Georgia Lee Lusk. Wikipedia.

Lusk, Georgia Lee. New Mexico's first woman congresswoman/educator. Georgia Lee Lusk has been called "one of the most influential educators in New Mexico," for her "resourcefulness, vision and integrity." Lusk was married to a prominent banker and cattleman who died in 1919. While raising her family alone, Georgia found time to serve twice as state superintendent of schools, where she worked for recodification of school laws, raising teaching standards, and championing consolidation of schools. A Democrat, she was elected to the US Congress in 1946. (1893–1971). *Notable New Mexico Women. Women in Education: New Mexico.*

MacMillan, Jesse. Solitary homesteader. After disembarking from the later ill-fated RMS Lusitania at Ellis Island, Jesse MacMillan detoured into nearby New York City to buy her first six-shooter. Thus armed, she boarded a days-long train trip by herself to New Mexico's south-central Sacramento Mountains to settle her homestead. The land had been secured by the Territory of New Mexico through land patent arrangement four years earlier. A privileged life in European boarding schools did not deter Jesse from working hard to introduce the first alfalfa crop in the area. In addition, she rode many miles on her horse "Wee Willie" to tutor local ranch children. (birth and death dates unavailable). New Mexico Historic Scenic Markers.

Madrid, Patricia. First woman New Mexico Attorney General. A former Latina Lawyer of the Year, Patricia Madrid views leadership as a means of empowering others. In 1998, she became the first woman elected Attorney General of the State of New Mexico. She was re-elected in 2002. (1947–). *Mujeres Valerosas ... meet the extraordinary women of the New Mexico Hispanic Women's Counci*l.

Petra Jiminez Maes.

Maes, Petra Jiminez. New Mexico's and nation's first woman State Supreme Court Justice. Petra Maes racked up many judicial firsts. She also was the first female Hispanic to serve on the high court. She was elected Chief Justice for the court twice, once in 2003 and again in 2012. Maes earned a Bachelor of Arts from the University of New Mexico and a Juris Doctor from University of New Mexico School of Law. (1947–). https://www.petrajm.com.

Alice Marriott. Wikipedia.

Marriott, Alice. Anthropologist and author. Alice Marriott helped popularize American Indian culture and the role of Native women through her book, *These Are the People: Some Notes on the Southwestern Indians,* Her work promoted an appreciation of their culture to a wider audience and helped eliminate the stereotype of Indians as uncivilized savages. "Indians are not beautiful, quaint and exotic creatures, like museum pieces," she once said. "They have a very rich and very complex culture with deep metaphysical and philosophical meanings." Her more than twenty books, including *Maria: The Potter of San Ildefonso* "were noted for reporting the unique culture of Indians with sensitivity while also portraying their universal humanity," observed her obituary in the *The New York Times. Alice Marriott Remembered*, edited and annotated for Sunstone Press by Charlotte Whaley, is her memoirs completed at age seventy-eight. (1910–1992). *These Are the People: Some Notes on the Southwestern Indians. Maria: The Potter of San Ildefonso. The New York Times*, March 21, 1992. *Alice Marriott Remembered.*

Marmon, Susie Rayos, Ga-wa goo maa (Early Riser.) Susie Marmon brought education back to the Laguna Pueblo. A lifelong teacher, oral historian, and storyteller, Susie Marmon devoted her life to her family and to her career as a teacher and educator of Native American children. It was rare for a Native American girl to pursue higher education at the turn of the twentieth century. In 1906, Susie did so, graduating from Bloomsburg State Teachers College, Pennsylvania. Her name references her proclivity for being a hard worker. In addition to raising a family with her husband of nearly fifty years, Walter Marmon, Susie taught Pueblo children in a one-room building behind her Laguna home. An oral historian, Susie told stories of the Laguna people. Those stories continue to inspire students of various heritages in the elementary school in Albuquerque that bears her name. Her life story exemplified the blending of two cultures; retaining the old, while learning the new. (1877–1988). New Mexico Historic Women Marker Initiative.

Agnes Bernice Martin.

Martin, Agnes Bernice. "Live as a verb, not as a noun." Iconic American minimalist abstract expressionist artist Agnes Martin worked into her nineties in a Taos retirement community. In doing so, she lived her credo: "We are born as verbs rather than as nouns. We are born to function in life, to work and do all positive actions that will carry out our potential..." Biographer Henry Martin (no relation) ranked her with "the great artists of the Twentieth Century." A Canadian, Martin received her bachelor's from Columbia University in 1942. In 1947 she attended the University of New Mexico's Summer Field School in Taos. She taught at the University of New Mexico before returning to Columbia for her master's degrees in 1952. Martin settled in Cuba, New Mexico, living there from 1968–1977 then in Galiseto for several years. One of her paintings was auctioned after her death for $13.7 million. (1912–2004). *Agnes Martin: Pioneer, Painter. Icon.*

Robin McKinney Martin

Martin, Robin McKinney. Newspaper owner and *Nueva Mexicana auténtica.* Born in Nambé, Martin began work while a teenager on her late father's newspaper, the *Santa Fe New Mexican.* Today she owns it. Martin filled numerous entry-level positions but also edited the paper's Spanish page. Later she was a reporter for the *Taos News*, a paper she acquired in 1978. She's been welcomed at pueblo feast days, then gotten up to help with the dishes. She has participated in *matanzas* and quizzed party-goers in Spanish about their families. An inductee in the New Mexico Press Association's Hall of Fame, Martin says "Everything I've done has been with other people's help." (1954–)

Agueda S. Martinez.

Martinez, Agueda S. Matriarch of New Mexico Hispanic weavers. Agueda Martinez was known for her complex designs and natural dyes. She was featured in the Academy Award-nominated documentary film *Agueda Martinez, Our People, Our Country.* At age twelve, Agueda's uncle began teaching her to weave wool rugs and blankets. She attributed her artistic gifts to her mixed heritage. Her great-grandfather was a Navajo weaver. Her ancestors also included early Spanish settlers. Her tapestries reflect both her Navajo and Spanish ancestry. At age eighteen, Agueda married a schoolteacher. She and her husband had ten children. For the first seventy-five years of her working career, Agueda is said to have completed a new weaving every day. Her work brought her many awards and recognition. In 1986, Agueda traveled to Washington, DC, with her daughter, granddaughter and great- granddaughter, to show their talents at the Smithsonian Institution. In 1992, one of Agueda's rugs was featured as the main design for the Institution's Festival of American Folklife. Agueda was honored again in 1993 by the National Women's Caucus for Art as its first Hispanic honoree for outstanding achievement in the visual arts. (1898–2000). New Mexico Historic Women Marker Initiative.

Martinez, Demetria. Award-winning author, activist, and journalist. "Involvement with something larger than myself compels me to write," says Demetria Martinez. Her widely translated novel *Mother Tongue* is based in part upon her 1988 trial for conspiracy against the US government in connection with allegedly smuggling Salvadoran refugees into the country. A religion reporter at the time, Martinez was covering the Sanctuary Movement involving American citizens who defied immigration law by aiding refugees fleeing Central America. A jury acquitted her on First Amendment grounds. The book won a Western States Book Award for Fiction. In *Block Captain's Daughter*, Albuquerque activists draw on the wisdom of their multiethnic/multinational roots in their struggle to better the world. It won a 2013 American Book Award and the International Latino Book Award for best Latino-focused fiction the same year. In 2013, she co-authored an e-book with former Oklahoma US Senator Fred Harris, *These People Want to Work: Immigration Reform.* It describes the plight of five undocumented women who live and work in the United States. *Confessions of a Berlitz-Tape Chicana* is a collection of autobiographical essays, including previously printed newspaper columns. It won the 2006 International Latino Book Award for best biography. Martinez has published poetry, *Breathing Between the Lines* (1997), and *The Devil's Workshop* (2002). She also co-authored a bilingual children's book, *Grandpa's Magic Tortilla,* with Rosalee Montoya. (1930–). www.demetriamartinez.com.

Esther P'Oe Tsawa (Blue Water) Martinez.

Martinez, Esther P'Oe Tsawa (Blue Water). Educator, linguist, storyteller. Esther Martinez's foremost contributions are documenting and preserving the Tewa language and the art of storytelling. Esther was named a National Heritage Fellow in 2006 by the National Endowment for the Arts. Esther was born in Colorado and later moved to live with her grandparents in Ohkay Owingeh Pueblo. She attended Santa Fe and Albuquerque Indian Schools, graduating in 1930. After graduation, she raised ten children and held cooking and cleaning jobs. From 1974 to 1989, Esther taught the Tewa language at the Ohkay Owingeh Pueblo. While working there, Esther met a linguist who asked for her help in documenting the Tewa language. This was the beginning of an important new phase of her life. Her great love for the native language of the Tewa led to many accomplishments. She was the first person to translate the *New Testament* into Tewa. She also published a collection of stories entitled *My Life in San Juan Pueblo - Stories of Esther Martinez.* Shortly before her death at age ninety-four, she received an honorary bachelor's degree from Northern New Mexico College. In December 2006, in recognition of her work, the Esther Martinez Native American Languages Preservation Act was signed into law. The act authorizes funding to assist tribes in preserving their heritage and culture. (1912–2006). New Mexico Historic Women Marker Initiative.

Maria Antonia Montoya, "Povika" (Flower Leaf) or "Poveka" (Pond Lily) Martinez. Women in New Mexico Collection, MSS 303, Box 1, Folder 83, Center for Southwest Research and Special Collections.

Martinez, Maria Antonia Montoya, "Povika" (Flower Leaf) or "Poveka" (Pond Lily). World renowned by accident. As Beverly West recounts in *More Than Petticoats: Remarkable New Mexico Women*, Maria Martinez of the San Ildefonso Pueblo and her husband Julian were firing her customary red pots one day when, fearing that the fire would become too hot thus ruining their work, she asked Julian to douse the flames. Grabbing the first thing that came to hand, manure, he threw handfuls of it on the fire until the flames were doused. To their astonishment, the pots had not cracked but had turned completely black. Maria quickly grabbed some black paint with which to decorate them and thus was born her famous black-on-black pottery. In keeping with her Pueblo's customs, Martinez taught her fellow potters the new method, and, "Through a happy disaster," West notes, "Maria Martinez had found a new form of pottery that would become accepted and popularized as her village's authentic, traditional pottery." West explains that Martinez had discovered a way to satisfy the Preservationists movement's appetite for authenticity while simultaneously facilitating the pueblo's "pursuit of cultural ability to grow and adapt to contemporaneous society." Maria teamed up with the director of the Museum of New Mexico, Edgar L. Hewett, to produce some of the world's finest pots, marked by invitations to show at the World's Fairs in Chicago, St. Louis and the Panama-Pacific Exposition in San Diego. (ca. 1887–1980). *More Than Petticoats: Remarkable New Mexico Women.*

Martinez, Susana. First elected woman governor of New Mexico. Susana Martinez served as thirty-first governor of New Mexico from 2011 to 2019. As such, she was the first elected woman governor of New Mexico and the first Hispanic woman state chief executive in the United States. The distinction is important. Democrat Soledad Chavez de Chacón preceded her in office in New Mexico nearly a century earlier but on an appointive basis. A Republican, Martinez served as chair of the Republican Governors Association from 2015 to 2016 and addressed the GOP National Convention. Martinez was succeeded by Democrat Michelle Lujan Grisham. Martinez began her working life as a security guard in El Paso in her family business. (1959–). https://ballotpedia.org/Susana-Martinez.

Susana Martinez.

McCarty, Frankie Gallegos. Excelled in a man's world. Frankie McCarty was a woman who spent forty years in the male-dominated world of New Mexico journalism and who racked up many firsts: the first woman to cover "hard news," the first to be named city editor of the Albuquerque Journal, and the first to become its managing editor. *Albuquerque Journal* publisher T.H. Lang appointed McCarty managing editor in 1976. She became one of the first women in the country to hold that position. "She was a groundbreaking journalist who cared deeply about the newspaper and her community," Lang said. "She mentored a whole generation of New Mexico journalists." McCarty won a wide variety of professional awards for her achievements. (1928–2005). *Albuquerque Journal*, October 27, 2005. *New Mexico Historical Biographies*. Ron Hamm.

Dorothy McKibbin. Los Alamos National Laboratory.

McKibbin, Dorothy. Gatekeeper of Los Alamos. Dorothy McKibbin was the first person to greet newly arriving scientists, workers, and their families on their way to "The Hill," the nearby top secret headquarters for the Manhattan Project in Los Alamos during World War II. Hired by Robert Oppenheimer as a secretary in 1943, her office in Santa Fe was the entrance and departure point for everyone who worked and lived at Los Alamos. McKibbin fostered a welcoming atmosphere by providing assistance, directions, reservations, or just a kind word. She played an indispensable role during the war and afterward remained the head of the Santa Fe office until she retired in 1963. She is remembered for her warmth and generous spirit. (1897–1985). New Mexico Historic Women Marker Initiative.

Medina, Gachupin Trinidad. Widely known potter of Zia Pueblo. Trinidad Medina used her ancestors' tradition of hand coiling clay in making her pottery. She became known for her large polychrome *ollas* (storage jars). Trinidad was invited to demonstrate her techniques throughout the United States. Sponsored by trader Wick Miller, she toured the United States from 1930 to 1946, demonstrating her craft at department stores and national exhibitions. By the time of her death, Trinidad had successfully passed on her knowledge. One of her students was daughter-in-law Sophia Medina. By then, Sophia had already been making and selling the traditional Zia ollas. Sofia ensured that Trinidad's legacy lives on. She and her daughter Lois began working as a team to produce the pottery and captured various awards. Trinidad's dream has been fulfilled. (ca. 1883–1969). New Mexico Historic Women Marker Initiative.

Christy Meta.

Meta, Christy, DO. Pioneer African-American osteopath. Christy Meta, the daughter of slaves, was the world's first African-American osteopath. She began her practice in Las Vegas, New Mexico, and practiced there throughout her lifetime. She is recognized by the American Osteopathic Association as the first black osteopath. Christy graduated in 1921 from the Philadelphia College of Osteopathic Medicine as its first black graduate. She began her practice in Las Vegas at a time when there were no women physicians or osteopaths in local hospitals and few blacks in the city. (1895–1968). New Mexico Historic Women Marker Initiative.

Miller, Darlis, PhD. Historian, author. Darlis Miller grew up with a lifelong love of the Girl Scouts and history. In 1964, she and her husband moved to Las Cruces where she first taught junior high school social studies. She later earned her master's degree and doctorate in history at New Mexico State

University (NMSU). In 1975 Miller began a twenty-four year career at NMSU. Following retirement, she continued to research historical topics and wrote several articles and books dealing with the American West and Southwest, including *Captain Jack Crawford: Buckskin Poet, Scout, and Showman* (1993), *Mary Hallock Foote: Author-Illustrator of the American West* (2002), *Matilda Coxe Stevenson: Pioneering Anthropologist* (2007), and *Open Range, The Life of Agnes Morley Cleaveland (*2010). She was active in the Western History Association, receiving its Award of Merit in 2011. (1939–2018). *Las Cruces Sun-News,* February 14, 2018.

Pamela Burgy Minzner.

Minzner, Pamela Burgy. Judicial pioneer. Pamela Minzner took Mary Walters's seat on the New Mexico Court of Appeals. Following Justice Walters to the New Mexico Supreme Court, Minzner became the first woman chief justice. Renowned for her "intellect, kindness, professionalism, and gentle spirit," Minzner mentored hundreds of women in the legal profession. As a result, women regularly serve on New Mexico's courts. Following graduation from Miami University, Minzner was accepted into Harvard Law School, one of only twenty-two women in a class of five hundred who graduated in 1968. Immediately after graduation, she married classmate Dick Minzner. She practiced law in Boston but after a few years the couple decided they wanted a warmer climate and moved to Albuquerque without ever having visited the city. Minzner joined the law school faculty of the University of New Mexico where she taught twelve years prior to joining the state Court of Appeals in 1984. She served from 1984 to 1994, becoming chief judge in 1993. In November 1994, Governor Bruce King appointed her to the New Mexico Supreme Court. In January 1999 her colleagues appointed her as the first woman chief justice of the New Mexico Supreme Court where she served for two years. In the general election in 2002, she was elected to an eight-year term and served as Senior Justice until her death in 2007. (1943–2007). https://nmhistoricwomen.org/location/pamela-minzner

Natachee Scott Momaday. American Association of University Women-New Mexico. "Natachee Scott Momaday." (1976). https://digitalrepository.unm.edu/nm_women_aauw/10.

Momaday, Natachee Scott. Helped bridge the gap. Natachee Scott Momaday helped Native American students function in their own and the white cultures. The materials she developed were based on a child's experiences. *Owl in the Cedar Tree* (1965) is a classic example. Natachee's husband was a Kiowa artist. Their son, Scott Momaday, is a Pulitzer Prize winning author. After service with the Bureau of Indian Affairs, the couple operated the Jemez Pueblo Day School, where she taught art. Her work, along that with that of her students, has been exhibited throughout the world. (1913–1996). Find A Grave Memorial.

Moore, Bessie M. A memorable year. Bessie Moore's first year of teaching in Raton in 1908 was one she would never forget. Assigned to a third-grade class, Miss Moore showed up bright and early on the first day of term with materials suitable for children of eight or nine years of age—stories, activities, and the like. Her forty desks were soon occupied, and still they came. As she looked about Bessie noticed with alarm that some desks were filled, not with children but with young men and women. This was the first school experience for these young people, and they did not want to miss it. Certainly, the fairy tales and childish games Miss Moore had planned would not be suitable for this bunch. That first year was truly an education for the novice teacher, as well as for the students. Not only were there eight weddings among the students in her class, but Bessie came to understand that some would occasionally be late or absent, sometimes because they were in jail. But it was a productive year all in all. Quiet and unassuming, Bessie exerted great influence on the lives and thoughts of those she taught. (1889–1969). *Women in Education: New Mexico*. Find A Grave Memorial.

Moore, Nellie. Clovis civil rights activist. Nellie Moore is credited with launching the civil rights movement in Clovis, New Mexico, in the early 1960s. To do so at that time required considerable courage for an African-American woman to challenge the conservative establishment in her city. Moore is cited for instigating investigations into alleged mistreatment of Clovis black residents encountered in the city's institutions. (Birth and death dates not available). *Noteworthy Black Women of New Mexico*.

Ada McPherson Morley.

Morley, McPherson Ada. Left a legacy. Ada McPherson Morley married William Raymond Morley Sr., an engineer for the Santa Fe Railroad who also managed the Maxwell Land Grant, one of the largest in US history. Their children were Agnes, William Raymond "Ray," and Ada Loraine "Lora." When William Sr. died on a business trip to Mexico in 1883, Ada unexpectedly became a widow with a young family. The next year, she married Floyd Jarrett, who convinced her to invest most of her inheritance in their ranch in Datil, New Mexico. He squandered much of Ada's estate buying land and cattle. By 1889, the money was gone and so was he. Ada was left to run the ranch and tend her children. By that time, Agnes and Ray were in their teens and assumed some of the responsibility. Together they turned their ranch into a smoothly-run operation. Ada sent young Agnes to Philadelphia for her education although she spent breaks and summers on the ranch. Agnes did well in school and later graduated from Stanford University. When Ada died, she left behind quite a legacy. A lifelong suffragist, she also worked for the Prevention of Cruelty to Animals and the Prevention of Cruelty to Children. Daughter Agnes wrote a popular memoir of the family's time on the ranch, *No Life for A Lady.* (1852–1917). New Mexico Historic Women Marker Initiative.

Neff, Francine Irving. Handled our money. Former US Treasurer Francine Neff, an Albuquerque native active in GOP politics for decades, was a dedicated party stalwart, talented organizer, and gracious wife and hostess. "For two cents, I'd join the Republican party," Francine Neff allegedly said to a friend in Albuquerque in 1964 when Barry Goldwater was running against Lyndon B. Johnson for President of the United States. Her friend promptly removed two pennies from his pocket, handed them to Neff, and then closed the deal by sending someone from the local Republican organization to her home that evening to register her Republican. Ten years later, Mrs. Neff was rewarded for her faithful support and hard work in the party she had joined for two cents when President Nixon nominated her for Treasurer of the United States. Neff was a political neophyte when she volunteered to campaign for Goldwater, but she rose to national committeewoman before being tapped by Nixon. She was the seventh woman to hold the post. (1926–2010). *The New York Times*, June 27, 1974. *Albuquerque Journal*, February 12, 2010.

Newcomb, Franc. Clear-eyed observer of the Navajo. Firsthand experience imbued Franc Newcomb with a deep understanding and appreciation of her Navajo neighbors. She believed "Navajos are people, not objects for study." Navajo shaman and friend Hosteen Klah became concerned that a serious illness resulted from her exposure to sandpainting ceremonies and powerful prayers. They agreed to a blessing ceremony for her. Newcomb believed "from that time on I was regarded as a member of the Navajo tribe." At that time, harsh and rugged field conditions were the norm, but this did not deter Newcomb. At times, dust storms would arise, roads would be rough, muddy, or washed out. At first, she rode horseback to nearby ceremonies, but those more distant presented problems. A car became a necessity since motorists were discouraged from driving after dark because it was thought evil spirits roamed in the darkness. Franc possessed a photographic memory. After sitting for hours, Newcomb drew what she recollected once the essence of the original sandpainting was absorbed by the patient, taken apart, and returned to the earth. During multi-day ceremonies, she spent nights sketching so she would not transpose symbolic elements from one day's sketch onto the next day's. Over time, she learned the Navajo language, developed a remarkable memory for symbol and color placement, and improved eye-hand coordination in her work. Newcomb was not trained as an anthropologist, ethnographer, or artist. She possessed neither the social standing of well-known collector Mary Cabot Wheelwright nor the academic credentials of anthropologist Gladys Reichard but developed long-term relationships with both. (1887–1970). *Navajo Neighbors.*

Noogle, Anne. Amelia was her hero. Anne Noogle wanted to fly since seeing Amelia Earhart in an air show. Noogle ultimately achieved her goal, flying as a pilot for the Women Airforce Service Pilots (WASPs) during World War II. After the war, Noogle became an instructor at the University of New Mexico. Noogle began a career in photography in her forties for which she won a Guggenheim Fellowship for documenting the aging process in women. The University of New Mexico awarded her an honorary doctorate. She wrote *For God, Country, and the Thrill of It: Women Airforce Service* Pilots *(WASPs) during World War II*, *Soviet Airwomen in World War II* and *Silver Lining*. (1922–2005). *Albuquerque Journal*, August 29, 2005. Wikipedia.

Nunnery, Frances Minerva. Never learned to grow old. Shaped by adversity and illness, Frances Minerva Nunnery as a girl knew only hard work and few frills. Driven to a fresh start in New Mexico as the mother of a nine-month-old and fleeing from an abusive husband in Colorado, Nunnery found a fresh beginning as she worked her way through a succession of jobs, including rancher, law officer, real estate broker, and nightclub owner. She preferred ranch life because it allowed her to be self-sufficient. Nunnery's success was based on her "willingness to undertake any job." Joan Myers, in *Pie Town Woman,* notes that Nunnery "could well serve as a model of determination and independence for us all." She was a woman "who knew who she was and never became conventional." As death approached at age ninety-nine, Nunnery had become the exact opposite of those who mistakenly believe women are frail and powerless. Instead, she was "a determined, ingenious entrepreneur [who defied] every stereotype about women." In her nineties, Nunnery moved to Silver City for a warmer climate but continued to dabble in real estate. "I've never got the hang of being old," she noted. "I've worked hard all my life, but work's always been my pleasure." (1898–1997). *Woman of the Century: Her Story in Her Own Memorable Voice. Pie Town Woman.*

Kathryn Kennedy O'Connor. Albuquerque Little Theater.

O'Connor, Kathryn Kennedy. Driving force behind New Mexico's first civic theater. In 1927 Kathryn Kennedy O'Connor moved from New York City, where she had been a professional actress, to Albuquerque seeking a cure for tuberculosis. She found it. With assistance from her husband and using Works Progress Administration (WPA) funds, they built the Albuquerque Little Theatre. It was the first civic theatre in New Mexico. She directed it for the next thirty years. O'Connor described her experiences in *Theater in the Cow Country.* (1894–1965). *Notable New Mexico Women.*

Georgia O'Keeffe. Courtesy of Nancy Reily.

O'Keeffe, Georgia. Happiness not a primary consideration. For Georgia O'Keeffe, staying occupied trumped happiness. "I do not like the idea of happiness—is too momentary—I would say that I was always busy and interested in something—interest [for me] has more meaning than happiness." Perhaps that is one reason why O'Keeffe was drawn to New Mexico. In *A Woman on Paper*, Anita Pollitzer, a friend of O'Keeffe's since New York City Art Student League days, wrote that O'Keeffe was "drawn to the austerity and mysticism of [New Mexico's] symbols: life as a struggle, sadness and resurrection. What had seemed sinister and strange to others ... had truth and meaning for her." O'Keeffe once remarked that "There's nothing abstract about those [her] pictures, they are what I saw—and very realistic to me. I must say I changed the color to suit myself..." Nancy Hopkins Reily provides another view of O'Keeffe's husband and mentor Alfred Stieglitz in *Georgia O'Keeffe: A Private Friendship, Part I Walking the Sun Prairie Land.* "She liked solitude to work, he liked company; he displayed an intellectualism, she intuitiveness; she loved the country, he the city; she wanted a child, he didn't.... Georgia needed space to flourish and her pioneering spirit provided the catalyst for...New Mexico." She is best known for painting large flowers and landscapes that had always enthralled her. O'Keeffe once said, "I painted the flower big to give the feeling I had in me when I looked at it." She wanted viewers to be "surprised into taking time to stop and really look." Animal skulls also figure prominently. "I painted my cow's head because I liked it and, in its way, it was a symbol of the best part of America I had found." (1887–1986). *A Woman on Paper, Georgia O'Keeffe: A Private Friendship Part I. Extraordinary Women of the American West.* New Mexico Historic Women Marker Initiative. *Notable New Mexico Women.*

Olivárez, Graciela. Untiring worker for Hispanic causes. Born to a Mexican-American mother and a Spanish father, Graciela Olivárez grew up in Arizona mining towns among Mexican American miners and their families. After dropping out of school, she moved to Phoenix where she worked as a secretary, engineer, radio personality, and program director for a Spanish-language radio station. By 1961, she began using her media fame to help Mexican-Americans in Phoenix. Until 1966, she sought ways to lower juvenile delinquency among Mexican-American youth. In 1963, Graciela organized a national conference on bilingual education. After the War on Poverty legislation was passed, President Lyndon B. Johnson appointed her to the National Advisory Council on Economic Opportunity. In 1966, she became director of Arizona's Economic Opportunity Office.

Graciela returned to school when Father Theodore Hesburgh, president of Notre Dame University, invited her to attend law school even though she lacked a high school diploma. In 1970, she became the first woman and the first Latina to graduate from its law school. Then Graciela served as director of the University of New Mexico's Institute for Social Research and Development and as a professor of law. She became director of planning for the State of New Mexico in 1975 and, in 1977, was nominated by President Jimmy Carter to direct the Community Services Administration. Graciela was the first Mexican-American woman to serve as a director of the Mexican-American Legal Defense Fund and later became its chairperson. As one of her lasting legacies, she created Channel 41 in Albuquerque, the first Spanish-language television station. (1928–1987). Wikipedia.

Nina Otero-Warren.

Otero-Warren, Maria Adelina Emilia, "Nina." Suffragist, educator, author, businesswoman. Nina Otero-Warren was descended from two New Mexico pioneer Spanish families—the Lunas and the Oteros—and was one of the first New Mexico-born women to become professionally and politically active. During her lifetime, she served as

Santa Fe County schools superintendent, inspector of the US Department of the Interior Indian Services, and director of literacy programs for the Civilian Conservation Corps and the Works Progress Administration. Otero-Warren homesteaded twelve hundred acres outside Santa Fe during the height of the Great Depression. Her best-known published work is *Old Spain in Our Southwest,* published by Harcourt Brace in 1936. Sunstone Press published a new edition in 2006 with extensive new supplemental material. The book describes her childhood and is a charming compilation of memoirs, anecdotes, historical accounts, and folktales that Otero-Warren hoped would serve as a teaching tool to educate non-Hispanic audiences while gaining approval, respect, and admiration for New Mexico's Spanish-speaking population. *Women in Education: New Mexico* notes that she was "without peer" in regard to calling attention to the conditions and needs of education in her state. In *Nina Otero-Warren of Santa Fe* published by Sunstone Press, Charlotte Whaley notes that "In many ways her [Otero-Warren's] life paralleled that of Santa Fe and New Mexico in the early years of the twentieth century." Nina viewed change as inevitable and proceeded to make it work for her. (1881–1965). *Old Spain in Our Southwest.* New Mexico Historic Women Marker Initiative. *Notable New Mexico Women. Women in Education: New Mexico. Nina Otero-Warren of Santa Fe.*

Parker, Mattie. Fostered education for Black children of Las Cruces. When Mattie Parker and her husband moved from San Antonio, Texas, to the North Mesa of Las Cruces in 1923, they quickly saw the need for a school for Black children in their new neighborhood. "[M]ost importantly, they unselfishly provided land and material" for its construction. Mattie Parker was also known for helping the poor, sick, and homeless. (ca. 1894–unknown). *Noteworthy Black Women of New Mexico.*

Susan Parks and children.
Gwyneth is standing. R. Dean Collection.

Parks, Susan, "Susie." Remained at her post. Nineteen-year-old "Susie" Parks operated the telephone switchboard in the dusty Mexican border town of Columbus, New Mexico, in 1916. She and her husband, Garnet, owned and published the *Columbus Courier* and lived in the back of its office. Susie, alone with infant daughter Gwen, awoke in the early morning hours of March 9, 1916, to sounds of gunshots and shouts of "Viva Villa!" She quickly discerned what the commotion meant. Pancho Villa's army was raiding her village. Susie bravely withstood the gunfire, using her switchboard to summon National Guard troops from Deming thirty miles to the north. Susie and her baby sustained wounds from glass and bullet fragments. Today, reporting an emergency is as simple as calling 911. One hundred years ago this was not the case. To make a call, one had to contact the operator on duty who placed the call through a switchboard. Susie had no idea that she would soon become a heroine. Leaping from bed, she picked up her sleeping infant and lit a match to find her way to the switchboard. But the light instantly attracted the attention of the raiders, making her a target. Bullets shattered the window, sending shards flying. Susie knew she had to get to the switchboard. Clutching the baby even closer, she crept low to the floor. Susie's first call was to Garnet, who was spending the night at their ranch outside town. He told her to call the National Guard. She hung up quickly and put a call through "Come quick!" she pleaded in a low voice. Then she unplugged the line and retreated with baby Gwen to a dark corner. The Deming operator apparently did not understand the unusual early-morning request and returned the call. That brought more shots. Crawling back to the switchboard in the dark, Susie again connected the line. This time she clarified the situation and warned the operator not to call back because the buzzing of the switchboard would attract more shots. Susie's heroic actions saved many lives. *(1895–1981). "Susan Parks: An Unlikely Heroine." True* West, October. 1982. Ron Hamm. New Mexico Historic Women Marker Initiative. *Buried Treasures: Famous and Unusual Gravesites in New Mexico History.*

Elsie Worthington Clews Parsons, Courtesy of American Philosophical Society.

Parsons, Elsie Worthington Clews, PhD. Unconventional feminist sociologist. Elsie Clews Parsons possessed a "dauntless spirit and inexhaustible energy." She used these to further the study of Pueblo culture and society in New Mexico. Parsons's privileged background helped underwrite both her work and that of many less fortunate colleagues. As Desley Deacon observes,

Parsons's work "helped change the way" Americans perceived the Pueblo peoples. Beverly West called her an "Interpreter of the Past and Inventor of the Future." An unabashed feminist and proponent of trial marriages, Parsons wanted to "kill" the nineteenth century so women could begin the twentieth. This eventually led her to break previously held taboos about unmarried men and women working together in the field. She believed the emergence of feminism from a modernist revolution in science, art, and morals was one of its most important aspects. "The twentieth century," she said, is "high time that women should shout." Parsons argued for equal rights among the sexes, pointing out that if women are to be "fit wives and mothers" they must enjoy the same opportunities for development as men. Parsons's subsequent work, *Religious Charity* (1913) was published under a pseudonym to avoid the notoriety incurred by her first book. Another book argued that sexual stereotypes are ingrained in childhood based on the treatment of children of different sexes and based on their games, books, and toys. Parsons was more interested in "inventing the future" than in destroying the past. Lois Palken Rudnick writes that after spending part of 1923–24 in Taos Pueblo and learning what tribal elders could reveal to outsiders, Parsons wrote of it. "[T]he furor of the tribe rose to such a height that the publisher could not release it west of the Mississippi." Such scholarship and fearlessness eventually led to Parsons becoming the first woman president of the American Anthropological Association. (1875–1941). *Elsie Clews Parsons: Inventing Modern Life. Daughters of the Desert. More Than Petticoats: Remarkable New Mexico Women. Mabel Dodge Luhan and New Mexico's Anglo Arts Community. New Mexico Lives: Profiles and Historical Stories. Notable New Mexico Women.*

Agnes Lawrence Pelton.
Courtesy of University of New Mexico Art Museum.

Pelton, Agnes Lawrence. Groundbreaking inspiration behind New Mexico's Transcendentalists. Agnes Lawrence Pelton was a modernist painter, who moved to the United States as a child from Germany. She studied art on both continents. Lured to Taos by Mabel Dodge Luhan, in Taos Pelton painted Pueblo people, desert landscapes, and still lifes. Her work evolved through three distinct themes: her early "Imaginative Paintings," art of the American Southwest people and landscapes, and abstract art reflecting her spiritual beliefs.. The *Albuquerque Journal* called her a "transcendent genius" and a "groundbreaking master." (1881–1961). *Albuquerque Journal*, September 29, 2019. Kathaleen Roberts.

Jesusita Acosta Perrault.

Perrault, Jesusita Acosta. Wrote New Mexico's first geography text. Jesusita Acosta Perrault's accomplishments are impressive. During her fifteen years on the New Mexico Board of Education, she wrote a widely used public school textbook on New Mexico geography entitled *New Mexico Geography*. Perrault became one of New Mexico's most influential women in early statehood days. After graduating from Silver City's Normal School in 1898, she married Charlie May. But her young husband soon died. Jesusita taught for several years around Silver City, followed by a brief stint in Chihuahua, Mexico. Jesusita returned to Grant County and in 1909 married Edward A. Perrault. She worked as a translator for the Selective Service in 1915 and in the early 1920s was Grant County Deputy Assessor. Widowed a second time in 1926, she entered politics as a Republican candidate for county school superintendent. In 1928 Perrault was named juvenile court and probation officer. In 1929 she became New Mexico Secretary of State. This position assumed extra significance when the lieutenant governor resigned. Perrault—the next in line—acted as governor on several occasions while the chief executive was away. In 1931 President Herbert Hoover appointed Perrault federal employment commissioner for New Mexico. She also served on the national board of the Alianza Hispano-Americana. (1880–1962). "Coloring Outside the Lines: Empowered women in territorial and early-statehood Silver City." *Desert Exposure,* March 2012 *Women in Education: New Mexico.*

Poling-Kempes, Lesley. Chronicler of adopted homeland. Lesley Poling-Kempes, through such books as *Ladies of the Canyons: A League of Extraordinary Women and Their Adventures in the American Southwest* and *The Harvey Girls: Women Who Opened the West*, writes of women of strength who led the way in New Mexico. In *Valley of Shining Stone: The Story of Abiquiu, Ghost Ranch* and her fiction Poling-Kempes provides the backdrop for their lives. As Poling-Kempes relates it, after moving to New

Mexico she began her new work of telling "the real and imagined stories of my adopted homeland." *Valley of Shining Stone: The Story of Abiquiu. Ghost Ranch.*

Pond, Margaret Prince, "Peggy." Peace warrior. Margaret Prince was from an established northern New Mexico family with military and government roots. However, Peggy never hesitated to follow her conscience and was an outspoken environmental activist with Greenpeace and Peace Action New Mexico. Pond was often seen at Friday lunchtime in her hometown of Santa Fe, protesting US military intervention and demanding an end to nuclear weapons. During the 1990s, she reached thousands of youths in the Los Angeles schools with her Greenpeace-sponsored multimedia message on protecting the world's oceans. The *Santa Fe New Mexican* called her the city's "strong voice for peace." Others termed her a woman who wanted to make a difference. Peggy organized and led large and historic demonstrations against ongoing wars and the nuclear industry in Santa Fe and Los Alamos. Peggy was arrested on several occasions during nonviolent actions. (1947–2011). https://peggyprinceblogspot.com. *Santa Fe New Mexican*, September 9, 2011.

Ramo, Jenny. Poverty warrior. The *Albuquerque Journal* has termed Jenny Ramo a "poverty warrior" for her work as executive director of New Mexico Appleseed, which fights poverty in New Mexico. Ramo says her passion is for "permanent and dramatic improvements for children and families...stuck in the cycle of poverty." Project Appleseed is a nationwide organization that encourages parental involvement in public schools. Ramo believes New Mexico has to focus on bipartisan and data-drive solutions to its poverty issues. *Albuquerque Journal,* February 9, 2020. Kent Walz. (birth, death dates not available).

Reebel, Mollie. Volunteer to New Mexico's native people. Inspiring tales of the contributions by community worker Mollie Reebel to New Mexico Native people are related in *New Mexico Recollections*. In 1929, Reebel acquired four goats and distributed their milk to undernourished babies at Jemez Pueblo. During her stay there, the infant and maternal death rates nosedived. The attractive and vivacious young woman also made quite an impression on the Jemez men. After Reebel left, she received a formal written proposal of marriage from one of them. Once on her new assignment at the Navajo reservation, she began her work by treating the horses and enticed tribal members to come to her house to use her sewing machine. The women were afraid of the contraption but not the men; who used it to sew their wives' wide traditional calico skirts (birth and death dates unavailable). *New Mexico Recollections.*

Reichard, Gladys Amanda, PhD. Anthropologist, linguist. Gladys Reichard, another devotee of Franz Boas, has been called "One of the most important women" to have studied Native American languages in the first half of the twentieth century. So says Betty Woods in *101 New Mexico Women and Men*. Reichard taught Navajos to read and write and compiled a grammar in their language. Her *Spider Woman* is rated a classic on Native American weaving. Some of her other writing includes *Social Life of the Navajo Indians* (1928); *Navajo Shepherd and Weaver* (1936); *Dezba, Woman of the Desert* (1939); *Navajo Religion: A Study of Symbolism* (1950); *Navajo Grammar* (1951). (1893–1955). *101 New Mexico Women and Men.*

Barbara Jane Awalt Rhetts.
Albuquerque Journal.

Rhetts, Barbara Jane Awalt. Publisher, author,"buy local" advocate. Barb Awalt was co-owner of Rio Grande Books and LTD Press and co-founder of the New Mexico Book Co-Op with her husband Paul Rhetts. She promoted local authors and was a champion of "buy local." The *Albuquerque Journal* called her an "indomitable force" in promoting local authors and bookstores. Slim Randles, whom Rhetts published, said Barb Awalt was someone he thought never needed assertiveness training and that she was "hell on wheels and a thorn in the side" of those she thought were taking advantage of others. Awalt helped guide hundreds of authors in their pursuit of getting published and distributed to local bookstores and readers. Her company grew to be one of the largest independent book publishers in New Mexico with almost three-hundred fifty titles in print. Awalt received many awards for her work. (1951–2019). *Albuquerque Journal*, May 26, 2019.

Richardson, Barbara. Advocate for New Mexico's Black community. Barbara Richardson served in many roles to advance the cause of African Americans in New Mexico. She wrote a preemployment guideline for minorities entering the workforce; developed a program to obtain jobs for Black ex-offenders; developed a human resources program for the state's African Americans; wrote three books; and was a lecturer and consultant. As a parent of five school-age children, she ran for the Albuquerque School Board, the first of her race to do so. All this, despite suffering from crippling arthritis. (birth and death dates unavailable). *Noteworthy Black Women of New Mexico.* (birth, death dates unavailable).

Riddle, Claudine. Realtor, activist, advocate for the Navajo. Born into a Texas sharecropper's family, Claudine worked hard her entire life. She is remembered for her no-nonsense attitude and fiery temperament that allowed her to succeed no matter the obstacles. 1920–2015. *Farmington Daily Times.*

Sally J. Rooke. Photo Folsom Museum.

Rooke, Sarah J., "Sallie." Resolute heroine. On the fateful day of August 27, 1908, as an unprecedented flood bore down on her hometown of Folsom, New Mexico, "Sallie" Rooke resolutely continued to operate her telephone switchboard, alerting her fellow townspeople of the impending danger. It was only too late that the crippled, elderly operator found herself trapped beneath the swirling flood waters of the Dry Cimarron River. Rooke drowned alone at her post. Although she is credited with saving forty families, she perished along with sixteen others. In a bizarre twist, Rooke's body was not found until nearly a year later. According to LaVerne Hanners in *Girl on a Pony*, two cowboys out scavenging for firewood came upon her mummified body entangled in some brush. Rooke's impressive grave marker erected by her fellow workers in the Folsom Cemetery honors her sacrifice with these words: "With heroic devotion she glorified her calling by sacrificing her own life that others might live." The marker was funded by more than 4,000 dimes contributed by telephone operators around the United States. (1843–1908). *Girl on a Pony*. Find A Grave Memorial. New Mexico Historic Women Marker Initiative. *Buried Treasures: Famous and Unusual Gravesites in New Mexico History.*

Susan Rothenberg. Koos Breukel, courtesy Sperone Westwater, New York.

Rothenberg, Susan. Painter, printmaker, sculptor, draughtswoman. Susan Rothenberg has achieved prominence through her iconic images of the horse, in which she synthesizes the opposing forces of abstraction and representation. Her early work—large acrylic, figurative paintings—came to prominence in the 1970s New York art world, then almost completely dominated and defined by Minimalist aesthetics and theories. The first body of work for which Rothenberg became known centered on life-size images of horses. The horses, along with fragmented body parts (heads, eyes, and hands) are almost totemic, like primitive symbols, and serve as formal elements through which Rothenberg investigated the meaning, mechanics, and essence of painting. Rothenberg's paintings since the 1990s reflect her move to New Mexico, her adoption of oil painting, and her new-found interest in using the memory of observed and experienced events (a riding accident, a near-fatal bee sting, walking the dog, a game of poker, or dominoes). These scenes excerpted from daily life, whether highlighting an untoward event or a moment of remembrance, come to life through her brushwork. (1945–). Art 21.

Olive Rush.

Rush, Olive. Illustrator, muralist, denouncer of war. Olive Rush was a descandent of a prominent Quaker Indiana family and graduate of Earlham College. For her, religion and art were "almost interchangeable." Her work denounced war in our country's major conflicts. Rush first visited New Mexico in 1914 and moved permanently from Indianapolis six years later. She attributed the move, in part, to the fact that "artists are spiritual adventurers and the strange beauty of the Southwest Country invites us to dare all things." She was an exponent of American Indian art and its artists, especially the young. Rush worked with prominent Native-American educator Dorothy Dunn and promoted major national exhibitions of young Native-American artists. Stanley L. Cuba calls her the "dean of women artists in Santa Fe," saying she was the city's first important woman artist. During the Great Depression, Rush executed several murals for the Public Works of Art Project throughout the Southwest. One was in the LaFonda Hotel in Santa Fe where she worked with prominent New Mexico architect John Gaw Meem. Rush believed that "the long, slow, and silent past is like the [New Mexico] sky overhead—potent, watchful, eternal." Jann Haynes Gilmore notes that, the more Rush learned about different religions and the philosophies of artists she admired, the more she found that the two were closely linked. "As I grow older in art and life, I do not find merely expressing myself worthwhile just as imitating nature seems trivial, but I paint when I feel the necessity of transmitting some strong emotion that I experience." Olive derived solace and sustenance from her garden. "One lovely thing about a garden," she remarked, "is the way one's friends enjoy it. And they shout with joy ...at the abundance of not flowers but of fruit."

Rush frequently held tea parties there, and, in times when commissions were slow or paintings not selling well, she partook of its bounty. Rush recounted one Thanksgiving with "many good things [to eat], with both fireplaces blazing and a great old snowstorm going on outside." (1873–1966). *Olive Rush: A Hoosier Artist in New Mexico. Olive Rush: Finding Her Place in the Santa Fe Art Colony.*

Sharman Apt Russell. Courtesy of Sharman Russell.

Russell, Sharman Apt. Nature and science writer, advocate of citizen science. Sharman Apt Russell recalls coming to southwestern New Mexico where she now makes her home because she and her husband wanted to "root into the land, to sink into the soil and sun." Doing so transformed her life and informed her writing. Topics include citizen science, living in place, archaeology, butterflies, hunger, and pantheism. Her titles include *Standing in the Light: My Life as a Pantheist, Chasing Tiger Beetles and Other New Ways of Engaging the World,* and *An Obsession with Butterflies. Within Our Grasp: Childhood Malnutrition Worldwide and the Revolution Taking Place to End It.* (1954–). *Ross Calvin: Interpreter of the American Southwest.*

Salazar, Lucy M. Political activist, advocate for the disabled. Lucy M. Salazar was a longtime aide to New Mexico Congressman Manuel Lujan Jr. and an advocate for the disabled. Salazar dedicated much of her life to helping others. She was active in Republican Party politics for half a century, serving as a delegate to two national conventions and working on numerous campaigns. Becoming involved in politics was a natural step for Lucy. She worked for Lujan during his 1969-89 congressional stint as well as during his tenure as secretary of the interior under President George H.W. Bush. Salazar was a member of the National Federation of Republican Women for two decades and co-chaired its 1995 national convention in Albuquerque. She also chaired a national organization that promotes art, education, and creative expression for the disabled. (birthdate unknown–2006). *Albuquerque Journal,* October 12, 2006.

Sammons, Harriet Belle Ramsden. Banker, benefactress. After Harriett Ramsden married George W. Sammons MD, in 1910, the couple moved from Connecticut to Farmington, New Mexico. "Doc" Sammons opened the town's first hospital. During the Great Depression, Harriet bought out the San Juan National Bank, keeping it solvent and continuing to approve loans. Thanks to her leadership, countless Farmington citizens were able to avoid bankruptcy. She became the first woman president of the First National Bank in Farmington. Harriet influenced hundreds of men who came to Farmington to work in the oil and gas industry to save their money for the future. (1876–1954). New Mexico Historic Women Marker Initiative.

Sawyer, Dessie. Went the men one better.. Dessie Sawyer reportedly could "cuss better and ride a horse better than a man," said the late Holm O. Bursum III who admired her despite political differences. Dessie's public service and unstinting work for the Democratic party led her into national politics because "that's where the fun is." She was just twenty years old when their daughter Fern was born to her and husband Uyless Devoe (D.V.) in 1917. Her second daughter Myrl followed in 1921. Dessie and her family moved to their ranch near Crossroads, New Mexico, in 1928. They lived a simple life and worked hard. Their small home did not have running water or electricity. All that changed dramatically in 1948 when oil was discovered on the ranch. While her love for ranching and being a wife and mother came first, Dessie was also active in community activities and public affairs. She was a National Democratic Committeewoman and became a well known political figure in New Mexico. Dessie was inducted into the National Cowgirl Hall of Fame in 1981 for championing the western way of life. (1897–1990). New Mexico Historic Women Marker Initiative. *Hobbs News-Sun*, August 30, 1990. Interview with Holm O. Bursum III.

Fern Sawyer. Cowboy Hall of Fame.

Sawyer, Fern. In her parents' image. Taught to ride at an early age, Fern Sawyer became an accomplished cowgirl. For Fern, the traditional gender roles did not apply. Instead, she became interested in rodeos and competitive riding while still very young. Always independent, she attended a rodeo in Madison Square Garden in New York City at age sixteen without her parents' permission. She was the first woman to win the National Cutting Horse World Championship and was a founding member of the National Cutting Horse Association. She was the first woman inducted into the Cowboy Hall of Fame and founded the Museum of the Horse in Ruidoso. Fern was inducted into the National Cowgirl Hall of Fame, which honored her for outstanding contributions in preserving western heritage. Like her mother, Fern held various leadership roles in Democratic politics in New Mexico. She served as a platform committee member from New Mexico during the 1968 Democratic Convention. A contradiction, Fern chewed tobacco and was known to swear on a regular basis; she was also quite feminine. She loved all types of fashion and perfumes. (1917–1993). New Mexico Historic Women Marker Initiative.

Sergeant, Elsie Shepley. Born to write. Elsie Shepley Sergeant was born into a writing family, leading her to become a journalist and biographer. In 1910, Sergeant wrote her first article, which she published in *McClure's Magazine* under the editorship of Willa Cather, thus beginning a lifelong friendship between the two. When the *New Republic* was founded in 1914, Sergeant became a contributor. In 1916, she published her first book, *French Perspectives*, a result of her extensive travels as the *New Republic's* war correspondent. In October of 1918, Sergeant was severely injured when her companion picked up a hand grenade that exploded. That experience resulted in *Shadow-Shapes: Journal of a Wounded Woman,* 1920. In that same year she moved to Taos on her doctor's advice. There she wrote about the Pueblo Indians and New Mexico until the mid-1930s, publishing mostly political commentary. In the mid-1930s, Sergeant reported on Pueblo social conditions and reactions to the Wheeler-Howard Act. In 1953, she published *Willa Cather: A Memoir*. (1881–1965). Find A Grave.

Sister Blandina Maria Segale. *Albuquerque Journal.*

Segale, Blandina Sister, Rosaister "Rosa" Maria. Future Saint? Diminutive in stature but fierce in spirit and determination, Sister Blandina Segale helped establish schools and hospitals in Santa Fe and Albuquerque in the late 1880s. Sister Blandina was awarded the first-ever teacher's certificate issued in New Mexico. Sister Blandina related her encounters with high churchmen, outlaws, warring Apaches, and crooked politicians in her book *At the End of the Santa Fe Trail.* Much of it was built around letters to her sister, also a nun. Some see Sister Blandina as "a saint for our time." At age seventy-seven, when she went to Rome to lobby for the sainthood of Mother Elizabeth Seton, a Cincinnati newspaperman wrote that "people say that Sister Blandina is saint enough herself, canonized by sixty years of faithful doing." She once remarked that "the genuine charity of [my] mission makes me forget the hardships attached to it." Since often there were no funds to support the projects assigned her, she was always seeking donations to support her work. She once famously remarked that "I am treasurer of an empty purse." She adhered to the dictum: "Do what you can for others in the position you find yourself. Leave the rest to God." If canonized, Sister Blandina likely will be a patron saint of poor children, immigrants, and health care and railroad workers, all groups she assisted through charitable efforts. (1850–1941). *At the End of the Santa Fe Trail. Cincinnati Magazine*, April 2, 2016. *Albuquerque Journal*, November 16, 2016. Oliver Uytterbrouck. *Notable New Mexico Women*.

Shaw, Lucy Lepper. Founded outdoor refuge for poor girls. Lucy Lepper Shaw wanted poor girls from the cities to enjoy the benefits of the outdoors. Shaw was the first women's investment counselor at New York-based Banker's Trust Company, but drew national attention for turning an abandoned work camp for young men into her vision of opportunities for young women from urban areas of the Southwest. In five years, 2,000 girls from New Mexico and Arizona, many from Hispanic families left destitute by the Great Depression, lived at a former Civilian Conservation Corps camp in south-central New Mexico's Capitan Mountains. There they became skilled in stenography, furniture restoration, flag making, colcha embroidery, and the performance arts. Shaw and her husband ran Camp Capitan on a shoestring budget, in spite of which it managed to outlive similar camps of the era. (1886–1974). New Mexico Historic Women Marker Initiative. *Ruidoso News*, June 2, 2017.

Anna O. Shepard.

Shepard, Anna O. Discovered link between pottery and anthropological puzzles. Anna O. Shepard contributed significantly to understanding the technology of Southwestern and Mesoamerican pottery. As a girl, Shepard began studying archaeology with her father. Her book *Ceramics for the Archaeologist* is the definitive guide to ceramic analysis. C.L. Keffer Nail has called Shepard the "mother of ceramics analysis," adding that she "is responsible for how we study ceramics." Shepard left her doctorate program at the University of New Mexico because her male adviser would not approve her thesis topic. "The fact that a man was getting in her way but still went on to make a name for herself is phenomenal," Nail wrote (1903–1973). *Albuquerque Journal,* October 6, 2019.

Shepardson, Mary Thygeson, PhD. Political interpreter for the Navajos. A latecomer to anthropology, Mary Shepardson's aim was to present "with understanding the conflicting opinions and interests" among the Navajos themselves. Her goal, she said, was to evaluate their problems within a broad framework. She did her undergraduate work at Stanford and studied at the Sorbonne and the London School of Economics. Shepardson earned her doctorate from the University of California at Berkeley. Shepardson, a cultural anthropologist, authored many books and wrote several scholarly papers. Her major books were *Navajo Ways in Government* and *The Navajo Mountain Community*. (1906–1997). *Daughters of the Desert. SFGate,* April 4, 1997.

Leslie Marmon Silko.

Silko, Leslie Marmon. Novelist, poet, short story writer, essayist. A recurring theme of Leslie Marmon Silko's writing is racial uncertainty, i.e., the stress between her white and Laguna Pueblo ancestry. Silko grew up at Laguna Pueblo and was educated at the University of New Mexico. Her formative years were spent in the state. As did her great-grandmother before her, so did Silko marry a white man. "At the core of my writing," she observes in *Yellow Woman* and *Beauty of the Spirit: Essays on Native American Life Today* is her attempt to identify what it is to be "a half-breed, or mixed-blooded person; what it is to grow up neither white or fully traditional Indian." Silko notes that, while there may be a concept of the "traditional Indian" or "traditional Laguna Pueblo person," in the end, she concludes that "I am only one being, one Laguna woman." In *The Turquoise Ledge*—part memoir, part family history, and part rumination on gemology—she reflects that the turquoise stones she finds near her home on the desert north of Tucson, Arizona, "command her attention [because] diversity is integral to the cultural diversity that ensures some humans will survive in the event of one of the periodic global catastrophes." (1948–). *Yellow Woman* and *Beauty of the Spirit: Essays on Native American Life Today. The Turquoise Ledge.*

Allyson Siwik. Courtesy of Gila Regional Information Project.

Siwik, Allyson E. Guardian of the environment. Allyson Siwik directs the Gila Resources Information Project, a nonprofit organization headquartered in Silver City, New Mexico. Its mission is to protect and nurture human communities by safeguarding the natural resources that sustain everyone and to protect natural resources by facilitating informed public participation in resource-use decisions. A biologist by training turned full-time advocate, Siwik sees the changes about her since first experiencing the Gila Wilderness more than two decades ago. Siwik recalls "[v]ast expanses of land blanketed by grasslands and dotted with small trees. [T]he bones of the earth" were exposed "from weathering from wind, sun, and rain. Wild fire had left behind blackened snags...Cactus and ponderosa pine would appear virtually side by side." Now, she believes hotter, drier conditions have brought high-intensity wildfires and associated flooding. (1965–). *Ross Calvin: Interpreter of the American Southwest*. Ron Hamm.

Jackie Morgan Everts Bancroft Spencer.

Spencer, Jackie Morgan Everts Bancroft. Larger than life. Few people impacted the quality of life in south-central New Mexico more directly than did Jackie Spencer. Fiercely private who gave generously of her vast wealth, Jackie was twice widowed. Her first husband, Capitan rancher Hugh Bancroft Jr., was heir to the New York publishing fortune of Dow Jones & Company. When he died in 1953, Jackie was thrust into the top one percent of America's wealthiest citizens. Rather than return to her native Denver and cosmopolitan life, she married again to the family doctor, A.N. Spencer, MD, and made a home in dusty, wind-whipped Carrizozo, New Mexico. Jackie loved the more civilized refinements of life—fine dining and travel, symphonies and dramatic musicals—as her creation of the Spencer Theater in Ruidoso, New Mexico, attests. Her love for theater and the performing arts was so strong that she saved for fifteen years to build the Spencer, her "little gem." Jackie ensured that what mattered most to her and those she cared about happened. She and Spencer built an addition to the local hospital and underwrote its operating costs. She also helped with construction of a new school building and equipment. She toured a camp for troubled boys, and, when the bus she was touring in broke down, she bought the camp a new one. Carrizozo children wanted a boxing program, so she bought them a professional ring. They wanted to bowl, so she built a recreation center. Ruidoso children wanted to ski, so Jackie underwrote their annual lift tickets. Jackie Spencer used her wealth for the benefit of her fellow citizens. (1925–2003). *Women in Education: New Mexico.*

Spencer, Maria Gutiérrez. Social justice advocate. Punished for not speaking English in school, María Gutiérrez Spencer devoted her life to righting wrongs through education. She taught at New Mexico State University and pioneered bilingual and bicultural education in New Mexico, founding Bicultural Orientation and Language Development (BOLD) in Silver City. This eventually evolved into a statewide training effort. Spencer was one of the first teachers of Spanish for native speakers. Gutiérrez used her experience and education to develop a curriculum for native speakers and non-native speakers of Spanish at Las Cruces High School. "From the time I was a child...she would explain to me the advantages I had and how the culture of poverty is not about economics, it's about how you see the world and how you plan your life, how you survive," says her daughter. Maria was a cancer survivor for fifty years but traveled worldwide to train teachers. (1919–1992). New Mexico Historic Women Marker Initiative. *Las Cruces Sun-News,* September 27, 2015.

Spiegelberg, Flora Langerman. First Jewish woman in New Mexico? Flora Spiegelberg liked to refer to herself as "the first Jewish woman in New Mexico." The claim likely was not true. Centuries before, Doña Teresa Aguilera de y Roche preceded her. What was accurate for Flora was her circle of important acquaintances in Santa Fe during the 1880s. It was then that she and her merchant husband entertained celebrities such as Generals Philip H. Sheridan and Ulysses S. Grant, President and Mrs. Rutherford B. Hayes, and especially her dear friend, Archbishop Jean Baptiste Lamy. Lamy was so taken with her that he had placed the word "Adonai" (Hebrew for God) over the main arch of his cathedral. She also founded one of the Territory's first non-sectarian schools and raised funds for its school building. Flora also started a Sabbath School for Jewish children in her home. (1857–1943). *A Quilt of Words: Women's Diaries, Letters & Original Accounts of Life in the Southwest. 1860–1960.*

Flora Langerman Spiegelberg.

Stanley, Carol (Caroline) Bishop. Elements of her transformation. What formed Carol Bishop Stanley? A hard-drinking, hard-gambling husband. El Rancho de los Brujos and Georgia O'Keeffe. As Lesley Poling-Kempes writes, "In the Southwest of the early twentieth century, where men and women alike found an atmosphere that was culturally and emotionally liberating, it is not...surprising that the first Anglo American to own part of...and then move onto the Piedra Lumbre [of northwestern New

Mexico] was a woman." That woman was Carol Bishop Stanley, a hands-on pobladora (resident)." Stanley was born on a Massachusetts island and trained and performed as a classical pianist before fleeing West when her family denounced her proposed marriage to a concert violinist. Next was a whirlwind courtship and marriage to handsome cowboy Richard Pfäffle. They owned and ran dude ranches before their marriage fell apart but not before Pfäffle won the Rancho de los Brujos (ranch of the witches) in a poker game. When Stanley moved into the crumbling old adobe, she became "the first Anglo woman ever to live at the Ranch of the Witches." Three years after Stanley moved in in 1931, the famous New York painter Georgia O'Keeffe showed up at her door. O'Keeffe became the next Anglo tenant and began painting her signature work there. (1879–1948). *Ladies of the Canyons.*

Matilda Coxe Stevenson. Wikipedia.

Stevenson, Matilda Coxe. First woman ethnographer of the Southwest. Unconventional, groundbreaking, liberated—all fit Matilda Coxe Stevenson. She was an unconventional anthropologist and ethnologist who worked in Zuni and other New Mexico Pueblos with her husband. Cheryl J. Foote calls Stevenson the Southwest's first woman anthropologist. Privately educated in chemistry and mineralogy, she abandoned those disciplines for ethnology, which she learned by writing up her husband's notes. Stevenson wanted to build a foundation upon which others might build because, in her words to John Wesley Powell, "I feel I can do the most for science in this way." (1849–1915). *Women of the New Mexico Frontier. Matilda Coxe Stevenson: Pioneering Anthropologist. Daughters of the Desert: Women Anthropologists of the American Southwest,* 1880–1980. New Mexico Historic Women Marker Initiative.

Stinson-Otero, Katherine, "Kate." Flew through the glass ceiling. In her late 30s, Katherine "Kate" Stinson-Otero settled down in Santa Fe to a more prosaic existence as a mother and an award-winning architect wife of fellow airman Miguel Antonio Otero, Jr. It was not always so. Kate was the fourth woman in the United States to obtain a pilot's certificate, earned at age twenty-one. That was just the beginning of her lifelong adventures in the sky. As a girl, Kate found she liked flying so much that she gave up her piano studies and decided instead to become an aviator. She was met with a series of rejections from possible instructors for flying lessons, but Kate was so good that she soloed after only four hours of instruction. She quickly became known as the "Flying Schoolgirl." On July 18, 1915, Kate became the first woman to perform a loop at a Chicago air show and subsequently performed the feat some five-hundred times without a single accident. Her daring and skill earned her international acclaim. In 1917, she performed before the emperor in Peking, China, as well as before equally large crowds in Japan. Kate volunteered to fly in combat in World War I after training US Army officers to do so. But she was forced to settle for driving a Red Cross ambulance. In Europe she contracted influenza which damaged her lungs. Her mantra was "a clean airplane is a safe airplane." (1893–1977). *Katherine Stinson-Otero: High Flyer.*

Stright, Mary Lodisa. Missionary teacher to the Jemez. Mary Lodisa Stright was a missionary teacher for the Presbyterian Church at Jemez Pueblo and Jemez Springs from 1882 until her death more than fifty years later. She taught generations of Pueblo children, many of whom went on to assume important roles in life. Mary Stright's journals create a picture of what life was like for a Pennsylvania girl set down in the unfamiliar environment of the Southwest. Her writing reflects initial prejudice against Indians, Mexicans, and the Catholic Church. Stright left the Pueblo to marry a local trader and stage coach operator. She remained active in her church until her death. (1857–ca 1945). *Presbyterian Church Overview – Jemez Valley History.*

Taugelchee, Daisy. Greatest of them all. Daisy Taugelchee is considered the most celebrated and greatest Navajo weaver of the twentieth century, winning Gallup Inter-Tribal Indian Ceremonial at Gallup, New Mexico for twenty-five years. Daisy overcame family tragedy and scant schooling to achieve her fame. Both her parents died when she was young. Her education consisted of only a few years in Indian schools in Albuquerque and Phoenix. Daisy is one of only two "Legendary Master Weavers" identified in Mark Winter's *The Master Weavers*. Daisy was so good that judges had to create a separate category for her work so other Navajo weavers would not be dispirited in trying to compete against her. The US Postal Service honored her in 2004 with a stamp bearing the image of one of her rugs. (ca. 1910–1990). *Navajo Times*, January 13, 2011.

Daisy Taugelchee.
Toadlena Trading Post.

Templeton, Lucille Corinne, "Rini." Graphic artist, sculptor, political activist. "Rini" Templeton was active in New Mexico and the Southwest, as well as Mexico, both as an artist and political activist. She was art director of the *El Crepusculo* newspaper in Taos owned by Craig Vincent, husband of famed musician Jenny Vincent. Templeton also contributed to the muckraking journal *New Mexico Review*, which attracted the writing of author John Nichols. Templeton worked for leftist political causes in Cuba and Nicaragua after the Cuban Revolution and the electoral victory in Nicaragua of the Sandinista National Liberation Front (FSLN). Although her name is not well known, Templeton's uncredited graphic arts work has been used on countless fliers, posters, and banners for the labor, feminist, and social justice movements. She frequently gave her work away for political causes. Also on the *El Crepusculo* staff was Jesusita Perrault, former New Mexico secretary of state and author of the state's first geography text. (1935–1986). https// www.encyclopedia.com/... Templeton-Rini-1935-1986. *Taos News*, March 23, 2017. Meg Scherch Peterson.

Tingley, Carrie Wooster. Children's hospital founder. As the wife of New Mexico Governor Clyde Tingley, Carrie Wooster Tingley used her position and influence, not to mention her considerable inherited wealth, to found a children's hospital which bears her name today. Carrie Tingley came to the New Mexico Territory in 1910, seeking treatment for tuberculosis. By 1937, she was the state's first lady and a strong advocate for sick and disadvantaged children. She established the Carrie Tingley Hospital for children with polio in present-day Truth or Consequences, New Mexico. The hospital moved to Albuquerque in 1981 where it continues to care for children and adolescents with complex musculoskeletal and orthopedic conditions and related issues. Carrie Tingley is one New Mexico governor's wife who made a difference. A warm account of her life can be found in *The First Ladies of New Mexico*. (1877–1961). New Mexico Historic Women Marker Initiative. *Notable New Mexico Women. The First Ladies of New Mexico.*

Carrie WoosterTingley.

Toledo, Juanita T. Pha-Wa-Luh-Luh (Ring-Cloud Around the Moon.). Helped restore lost art of Pecos pottery. Juanita Toledo was born in 1914 in Jemez Pueblo as a direct descendant of the Pecos Pueblo people. Working with supporters of their craft, principally Evelyn M. Vigil un-pha-kee (Young Doe) these determined Pecos Pueblo women brought back the lost art of the Pecos Pueblo pottery and Pecos style glaze, thus making a major contribution in the history of Pueblo pottery. (1914–1999). New Mexico Historic Women Marker Initiative.

Joann Soge Track.
The Art Farm.

Track, JoAnn (Joann) Soge. Poet, children's author, photographer. A resident of Taos Pueblo, Joann Soge Track writes poetry and children's stories, and is an amateur photographer. Track believes her culture, her family, and home inspire her art. Track's work includes "Seven Directions," published in *Anthology of American Indian Writers* and "Clearing in the Valley" appearing in *Spider Woman's Granddaughters*. Track directed the film *Peabody Coal Company*, a documentary about the Peabody Coal Company of Black Mesa, Arizona. She also wrote *Tiwa Tales for the Taos Children's Theatre* and directed *Sesame Street* at the Taos Pueblo filmed by

The Children's Television Workshop. Track told Jane Katz of *Messenger of the Wind: Native American Women Tell Their Life Stories*; "It is our strong sehse of ceremony and ritual that keeps my people together." (ca. 1949–). *Messenger of the Wind: Native American Women Tell Their Life Stories.* The Art Ranch, Hot Springs CA.

Clara D. True.

True, Clara D. Reformer, militant feminist. Clara True acquired the sobriquet "feminist of the militant type" from noted anthropologist Elsie Clews Parsons. According to anthropologist Barbara Freire-Marreco Aitken, True was known by some government officials as the "She Devil of the Rio Grande" for her uncompromising belligerent attitude toward them in pursuit of her educational policies. Aitken called True "strong-willed and determined." True reputedly felt ill at ease with white men and avoided them when possible. A former Indian Bureau teacher and deputy commissioner turned horse trader and rancher, True employed Native hands only on her Pajarito Plateau ranch north of Santa Fe, which she shared with her mother and a woman friend. True and Mary Dissette, two of the most vociferous opponents of Pueblo dances in the 1920s, had taken up the call for women's work among Native Americans. True became involved in Indian reform in the 1890s when she served as principal of a boarding school on the Sioux Reservation. From 1902 to 1907, she taught at the Santa Clara Pueblo, and, in 1908 became superintendent of the Morongo Reservation in California. Around 1910, she returned to New Mexico to settle in the Española Valley near Santa Clara Pueblo. There she owned and operated ranches and managed an apple, hay, and livestock business. Although True did not work in an official capacity with them, she later involved herself intensely in affairs of the Santa Clara people. True once famously declared that, "I'll make the Indians save themselves." (1868–1950). *Elsie Clews Parsons: Inventing Modern Life. Making Savages of Us All: White Women, Pueblo Indians, and the Controversy over Indian Dances in the 1920s,* Margaret D. Jacobs University of Nebraska, Lincoln December 1996. *A Life Well Led. The Biography of Barbara Freire-Marreco Aitken, British Anthropologist.*

Maria Varela.

Varela, Maria. Organizer, activist, photographer. A teacher at the University of New Mexico, Varela worked in northern New Mexico in various civil rights capacities. One was organizing sheep growers to form a cooperative enterprise to revitalize the area's agricultural economy. Active in the civil rights movement since student days, Varela also made her voice heard alongside firebrand Reies Lopez Tijerina against outside land development in northern New Mexico. She also organized a medical clinic in tiny Los Ojos, New Mexico. Varela was formed in her work by her experience as a Student Non-Violent Coordinating Committee (SNCC) staff member from 1963 to 1967, working first in Selma, Alabama, and then across the Black Belt South. Raised Catholic by her Mexican father and Irish mother, Varela first got involved in the Catholic social justice movement by joining the Young Christian Students (YCS) in high school and then again in college. After graduation, Varela was recruited in 1961 to serve as a college campus organizer for the YCS National Office. She traveled across the country, urging Catholic students to support the Civil Rights Movement and especially sit-ins. (1940–). *Three Weavers.*

Martha Vázquez.

Vázquez, Martha. Judicial trailblazer. Martha Vázquez was the first woman judge in New Mexico, first woman to serve as Chief Judge of the United States District Court for the District of New Mexico, and the first Hispanic woman to serve as chief judge in the United States. A Notre Dame Law School graduate, Vázquez attributes her achievements as far back as the first day of grade school where she was singled out for not knowing English. That day remains for her the day she "understood nothing" and the moment she resolved to succeed. "Humiliation can make you angry," she observes, "or it can make you determined." She chose the latter. (1953–). *Mujeres Valerosas...meet the extraordinary women of the New Mexico Hispanic Women Council.*

Velarde, Pablita, Tse Tsan (Golden Dawn). Leading Native American artist. After being sent from her native Santa Clara Pueblo to Santa Fe for schooling, the young Pablita Velarde was fortunate to come under the tutelage of Dorothy Dunn and Olive Rush, supporters of young Native artistic talent. They were to have considerable influence on her life and career. With their encouragement, she began entering her work and earning recognition in increasingly important exhibitions. Velarde also executed a series of paintings at the Bandelier National Monument. Following her marriage in World War II, she had two children—one the equally acclaimed Helen Hardin. Despite her own considerable accomplishments, Velarde was engaged in a contentious relationship with Hardin until the former's fatal illness. Velarde's fame perhaps led to her celebrated book *Old Father Story Teller.* The book's goal is to preserve some of the oral myths of Santa Clara as Velarde heard them in childhood. Velarde wrote that she was "one of the fortunate children of my generation" who were probably the last to hear firsthand stories from Great-grandfather or Grandfather. Among Velarde's most prestigious awards is the *Ordre des Palmes académiques* bestowed by the government of France. (1918–2006). *Pablita Velarde: The Story of an American Indian, Old Father Story Teller.* New Mexico Historic Women Marker Initiative. *Notable New Mexico Women.*

Viarrial, Feliciana Tapia. Matriarch of Pojoaque Pueblo. As a girl, Feliciana Viarrial experienced her share of hard times. But her strong and persevering spirit proved beneficial not only for her family but also for her Pueblo of Pojoaque. The modern Pueblo of Pojoaque or Posuwageh, "water drinking place," is a Tewa village that was founded around 900 AD. By 1913, it was apparent that the families living there were not going to be able to survive their economic hardship. Most left, including Feliciana and her family, seeking work in Colorado and Utah. Feliciana attended the Santa Fe Indian School from the age of six to sixteen as an honor student. After her education, she returned to her family in Colorado. There she met and married and started a family. In 1932, Feliciana's father learned that the Bureau of Indian Affairs was seeking heirs of the Pueblo of Pojoaque. He decided to lead fourteen family members home. Feliciana returned with her family to begin rebuilding the pueblo. She was a loving wife and mother of twelve. With all of her other responsibilities, Feliciana managed to play a significant role in leading the Pueblo from near extinction to becoming the cultural center and economic power it is today. (1904–1988). *Mujeres Valerosas...meet the extraordinary women of the New Mexico Hispanic Women Council.* New Mexico Historic Women Marker Initiative.

Vigil, Evelyn M. Un-Pha-Kee. (Young Doe). Descendant of Pecos people. Evelyn Vigil was born in 1921 in Jemez Pueblo. She is a direct descendant of the thirty-eight people from the now extinct Pecos Pueblo who moved to Jemez Pueblo in 1828. Evelyn collected clay and natural paint pigments around Pecos and found the old grindstones near their source. She promoted a revival of her ancestors' pottery dating between 1250 and 1700. (1921–1995). New Mexico Historic Women Marker Initiative.

Rebecca Vigil-Giron. Wikipedia

Vigil-Giron, Rebecca. Not just a man's world. Rebecca Vigil-Giron is the three-time and longest-serving New Mexico secretary of state. Born and raised in Taos, New Mexico, Vigil-Giron is an 11th generation New Mexican and was educated at Highlands University in Las Vegas, New Mexico. She has been a reform consultant in the Dominican Republic, Nicaragua, and parts of Africa. Vigil-Giron was instrumental in the implementation of the Help America Vote Act. Rejecting the idea that she "as a woman inhabits a man's world," she counters, "This is my world, and I take advantage of every opportunity placed before me." (1954–). *Mujeres Valerosas...meet the extraordinary women of the New Mexico Hispanic Women's' Council.* Ballotpedia.

Emiteria Martinez Robinson "Matie" Viles.
Courtesy of Meredith Hmura.

Viles, Emiteria Martinez Robinson, "Matie." Unheralded benefactress. Perhaps because she was orphaned as a child and was taught to steal food in order to eat, Emiteria "Matie" Viles would forever have a special feeling toward orphans. Matie married George A. "Skipper" Viles in 1908. When he found work at a lodge near Cowles, New Mexico, Matie packed their belongings on two buckboards and navigated rough terrain to get there and then to help him run the enterprise. In 1930, the couple bought Mountain View Ranch, a dude ranch patronized by East Coast investors who quietly gave Skipper financial advice. He listened but kept his own counsel. Skipper, according to biographer Merideth A. Hmura, had "a keen knowledge of the market." He lived by the stricture "don't spend your money until you have increased it." When Skipper died, Matie believed she did not have enough money for his funeral. However, he had kept secret a fortune amassed through investments. Upon learning of her sudden wealth, Matie established the Viles Foundation, celebrating its fiftieth anniversary in 2019, to provide college scholarships for orphans and youth in San Miguel and Mora Counties. By then, the Foundation had granted nearly $3 million to 961 students statewide, many of whom achieved success in their careers and lives. (1888–1961). New Mexico Historic Women Marker Initiative. www.vilesfoundation.org. *Mountain View Ranch.*

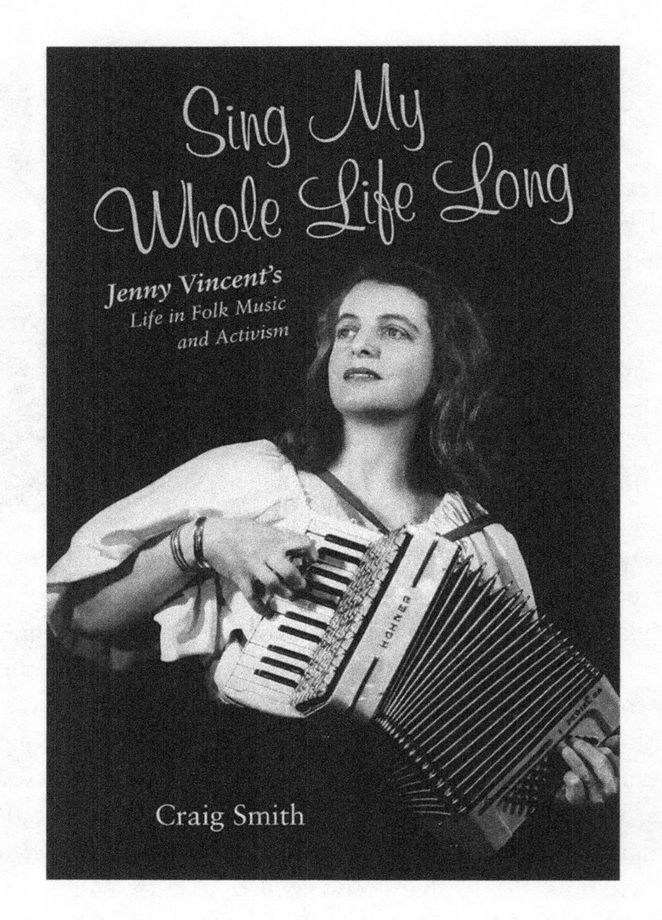

Jenny Wells Vincent. Courtesy of University of New Mexico Press.

Vincent, Jenny Wells. Rocky Mountain thrush. Following graduation from Vassar in 1936, Jenny and husband Dan Wells visited the San Cristóbal, New Mexico, ranch of D.H. Lawrence's widow Frieda and moved there. The couple founded a school for youngsters because Jenny, a classically trained musician, believed in "the power of music for the people." Jenny began visiting schools where she played Mexican folk songs, often singing them in Spanish, counter to the wishes of school administrators who forbade speaking Spanish. In 1943, she joined the Rocky Mountain Farmers Union, which Jenny considered "a milestone" for her personal and political maturation. That was followed by membership in the Communist Party. "No political decision she ever made would have a more lasting or tumultuous effect on her life," wrote biographer Craig Smith. After divorcing Wells, Jenny married Craig Vincent. They converted the school to a guest ranch, "not to raise livestock" but to "foster a community among progressives looking for a refuge from the battles of the Cold War." The Vincents became involved in several political and social causes, including the Salt of the Earth mine strike in Grant County, New Mexico. Believing that music was an avenue for social advocacy, Jenny began performing with like-minded musicians such as Pete Seeger, Paul Robeson, and Woody Guthrie. As she aged, Jenny entered a rest home in Taos and entertained fellow residents until her death at age one-hundred and two. Her commitment and success in preserving the rich legacy of Spanish-language songs of the Southwest was among her singular accomplishments. Novelist John Nichols has called her "a candle burning brightly in the hurricane...." (1913–2016). *Taos News,* May 9, 2016. *Sing My Whole Life Long.*

Waconda, Josephine T., Rear Admiral. A career of firsts. Josephine Waconda, a member of the Laguna and Isleta Pueblos, was the first Native-American woman to attain the rank of rear admiral in the US Public Health Service (PHS). In 1955, Waconda earned her bachelor's of nursing degree from the University of New Mexico (UNM) in 1975 and became an officer in the PHS Commissioned Corps the following year. Since her work was in small rural New Mexico clinics, Waconda decided to become a nurse practitioner and returned to school where she became UNM's first Native-American woman to graduate as a Certified Nurse Practitioner (CNP). In 1987, she was named assistant surgeon general and was promoted to rear admiral. During her career, Waconda managed a varied health-care program that covered 76,000 Native Americans in four states and more than twenty-five Pueblos and tribes through five hospitals, a regional treatment center, twelve health centers, and seven health stations. She established the first diabetes clinics in the Indian Health Services, initiated some of its first wellness programs and teen clinics, and implemented child abuse prevention and suicide prevention task forces. Waconda termed her PHS service "the most rewarding " of her career. "The Native Americans in New Mexico are my people and have been the focus of my career," she reflected. (1935–2013). The FreeLibrary.com. *Buried Treasures: Famous and Unusual Gravesites in New Mexico History.*

Mary Coon Walters.

Walters, Mary Coon. From Women Airforce Service Pilots (WASP) to the bench. As one of fifty-nine women who graduated from the WASP training program in 1943, Mary Coon was a transport pilot during World War II and the Korean Conflict. Later, she flew for a rancher in Texas. By this time, she was married to Asa Lane Walters, and they had a son. Mary, who had a degree in Home Economics, decided to take advantage of the GI Bill and attend the University of New Mexico Law School. She graduated at age forty and was admitted to the State Bar of New Mexico in 1962. Soon Mary became a leader in the New Mexico legal community. In 1969, she was a delegate to the New Mexico Constitutional Convention. After practicing law for nine years, she became the first woman judge named to the District Court in Albuquerque. Mary was subsequently elected to the New Mexico Court of Appeals, serving from 1978 to 1984, becoming its first woman chief judge. In 1984, Mary also was the first woman appointed to the New Mexico Supreme Court. She received many awards throughout her lifetime, including induction into the New Mexico Women's Hall of Fame. Throughout her career, she served on the Judicial Liaison Committee and the Governor's Commission on Criminal Justice Planning. Mary was also the first president of the New Mexico Women's Political Caucus. She inspired many New Mexico women in the field of law. (1922–2001). New Mexico Historic Women Marker Initiative.

Edith Warner and companion Adelano (Tilano) Montoya.
Atomic Energy Foundation.

Warner, Edith. Bridge between cultures. Self-effacing and quiet, Edith Warner was a neighbor to both the brilliant scientists who developed the atomic bomb at the Los Alamos National Laboratory and to her close Native American neighbors at San Ildefonso Pueblo. Her particular friend and companion was Tilano Montoya. Edith was the subject of *The House at Otowi Bridge*, *In the Shadow of Los Alamos: Selected Writings of Edith Warner*, and a historical novel by Frank Waters, *The Woman at Otowi Crossing*. Edith lived in a humble dwelling by the side of the road on the banks of the Rio Grande, and often "stood on the riverbank to pray." She knew the ancient ones were wise to pray for peace and beauty and not for specific gifts except fertility, "which is continued life." For her, the "song of the river" was an enduring solace. It always made her feel "very near the source of things." Edith came to New Mexico in 1922 after experiencing a near nervous breakdown. She became friends with Maria Martinez, the famed potter and the equally famed Danish physicist Niels Bohr. Like her Native American neighbors, Edith knew better than her scientist friends of the frailties of the land. "My friend was wrong who said that this country was so old it does not matter what we Anglos do here," she wrote. "What we do anywhere matters but especially here. It matters very much." During the dark days of World War II with many of the sons of her pueblo neighbors off to war, she began a series of "Christmas Reports." Edith further recounted that "After the fears and confusion of 1943, this year's peace and beauty stand out like shining peaks." Edith added that: "[i]t matters not that the color of skin be different, that language be not the same, that even the gods of our fathers be known by a different name. We are people, the same kind of human beings who live and love and go on ..." In her nearly thirty years beside the river, Warner developed a simple philosophy that led her to a oneness with the earth, not dissimilar to her Pueblo friends. (1893–1951). *The House at Otowi Bridge. In the Shadow of Los Alamos: Selected Writings of Edith Warner. The Woman at Otowi Crossing.*

Elizabeth Warren (right) discusses office affairs with secretary Carrie Lynnfoot. Courtesy of Silver City, New Mexico Museum. Image 11889.

Warren, Elizabeth. Ultimate role model for female empowerment. Among other activities, Elizabeth Warren was a real estate investor and contractor in Silver City, New Mexico, in the late nineteenth and early twentieth centuries. Assisting her husband in running his businesses was the avenue through which Elizabeth entered the public sphere where she would long occupy a prominent position. At age nineteen, she married Orange Scott Warren. After traveling extensively as a couple, Warren came to Silver City in 1882 and started an insurance business. Elizabeth traveled to New Mexico from San Francisco by stagecoach with her three young children to reunite the family. When her husband died suddenly in 1885, Elizabeth secured an appointment as agent for the companies he had represented. She excelled, eventually buying out several competitors. Expanding into real estate, Elizabeth acquired many properties and converted a mining boom-era hotel into a luxury resort for health-seekers. After the devastating Silver City 1902 flood, she oversaw construction of a massive stone wall to shore up her home and office, the only historic Main Street building to ultimately survive. Her activities expanded to include sidewalk construction when a 1907 ordinance required property owners to install concrete sidewalks. "Mrs. O. S. Warren and Mrs. F. J. Wright were the first firm of women contractors in these United States," noted the *Silver City Independent* in March 1920, adding that "these sidewalks will still be here and still be serviceable when the present generation and several others are gone." In 1892 a local newspaper noted talk of nominating "ladies" for the office of county school superintendent, something that had apparently been tried elsewhere. Warren was suggested. One editor candidly remarked, "Mrs. Warren was really the first superintendent Grant County ever had, as she did the work while her husband, Mr. O. S. Warren, filled the office." (1855–1945). "Coloring Outside the Lines: Empowered women in territorial and early-statehood Silver City." *Desert Exposure*, March 2012.

Annie Dodge Wauneka.

Wauneka, Annie Dodge, PhD. A voice for the Nation. Annie Dodge Wauneka was the first woman representative on the Navajo Nation Tribal Council. She became a strong advocate for the improved health and education of her people. The Council established its first college scholarship program under her leadership. Although she was not a trained educator, Wauneka spoke throughout the reservation and hosted a weekly radio program in which she urged her people to accept modern medicine and better nutrition. At that time, many Navajos did not read, but they did trust what Wauneka had to say. Her work was a major factor in reducing tuberculosis in the Navajo Nation. Wauneka also worked for equal rights for women, including status, identity, employment rights, and housing. She won numerous awards for her work. (1910–1997). New Mexico Historic Women Marker Initiative. *Notable New Mexico Women. Women in Education: New Mexico.*

Marta Weigle. University of New Mexico.

Weigle, Marta, PhD. Scholar, prolific author. Marta Weigle is recognized for her contributions to New Mexico scholarship and for preserving history through co-founding Ancient City Press in Santa Fe. Weigle came with her family to New Mexico at age seventeen After earning her doctorate in folklore and folklife from the University of Pennsylvania, she entered teaching at the University of New Mexico in 1972, where she remained for almost forty years. The *Santa Fe New Mexican* called her "one of the great scholars of New Mexico history and culture in the latter twentieth century." Her first major book, *Brothers of Light, Brothers of Blood: The Penitentes of the Southwest*, grew out of her doctoral dissertation. A strong feminist, Weigle published significant work on women and mythology. She is often cited for her "meticulous and prolific scholarship." (1944–2018). *Santa Fe New Mexican*, June 22, 2018.

Margaret Werner-Washburne.

Werner-Washburne, Margaret, PhD. Internationally known in yeast genomics. Daughter of a mother who had fled the Mexican revolution, Margaret Werner-Washburne returned to Mexico to better understand her roots. While there, she became interested in the use of medicinal plants. A former University of New Mexico professor, Werner-Washburne believes her "most lasting and important contribution" will be the hundreds of students to whose careers she contributed. "I love helping students develop their creativity, motivation and inspiration by listening to their own hearts and minds." She thinks this "propels them steadily forward and allows them to hold onto the fundamentals of who they are." Werner-Washburne has served as president of the Society for the Advancement of Chicanos/Hispanics and Native Americans in Science (SACNAS) 2013–2015. *Mujeres Valerosas...meet the extraordinary women of the Hispanic Womens Council.* "5 Things About Me" American Association for the Advancement of Science, retrieved October 17, 2018.(birth and death dates not available).

Mary Cabot Wheelwright.

Wheelwright, Mary Cabot. Enduring legacy. Mary Cabot Wheelwright's enduring legacy is the Wheelwright Museum of the American Indian in Santa Fe. Wheelwright believed "any fundamental success in creating something has to come from a certain fire." Creation of the museum bearing her name is evidence of that "certain fire." This she accomplished in collaboration with Navajo medicine man Hosteen Klah who feared his people's ways were vanishing. He joined forces with the wealthy, aristocratic

Boston Brahmin to preserve them. Wheelwright's role, in addition to providing financial support, according to Lesley Poling-Kempes in *Ladies of the Canyons,* was to preserve the Navajo's stories and rituals. This pursuit was to become "a consuming passion" that occupied Wheelwright for the rest of her life. Her resolve was strengthened, she noted in her unpublished autobiography *Journey Towards Understanding*, when—upon meeting Klah for the first time—she observed in him a "calm and benign" presence. "I got a very strong impression of power from him." Wheelwright hoped to find "freedom from the two curses of civilization: loneliness and boredom." As Sharon Niederman puts it in *A Quilt of Words: Women's Diaries, Letters & Original Accounts of Life in the Southwest, 1860–1960,* Wheelwright's lifelong spiritual quest was to become "a do-it-yourself ethnologist." (1878–1958). *A Quilt of Words: Women's Diaries, Letters & Original Accounts of Life in the Southwest, 1860–1960. Journey Towards Understanding. Ladies of the Canyons*. New Mexico Historic Women Marker Initiative.

White, Amelia Elizabeth. Combined archaeology and music. Amelia Elizabeth White had a keen interest in archaeology, as well as a strong interest in music. She played the piano and harpsichord and started the Santa Fe Sinfonietta and Choral Society. She worked tirelessly to promote Native-American art and to preserve Santa Fe's heritage. A philanthropist and community activist, White donated land for the Laboratory of Anthropology and the Wheelwright Museum, gave the city its first animal shelter, and established the Garcia Street Club for children. Her estate, once a gathering place for local artists, is now home to the School for Advanced Research. (1878–1972). New Mexico Historic Women Marker Initiative.

White, Elizabeth Boyd **(See Boyd, E.)**

White, Mary. Early New Mexico Girl Scout leader. In 1927, "Miss Mary" White established one of the earliest Girl Scout camps in America and the first in New Mexico. Situated on two hundred acres in Otero County, the camp honors its founder by bearing her name. Generations of New Mexico girls have learned stewardship of nature and community at the camp and continue to be energized as activists by Mary White's pioneer spirit. In 1923, President Harding appointed Mary to become the acting postmistress in Chaves County—a position she held until 1931. It was also in 1923 that Mary became one of the earliest leaders of the Girl Scout movement, when she helped launch the first Girl Scout troop in Roswell. (1894–1988). New Mexico Historic Women Marker Initiative.

White, Rose Powers. Tireless worker to preserve history. Rose Powers White worked tirelessly to compile histories of early southeastern New Mexico pioneers. Rose was president of the New Mexico Folklore Society and, with her husband R. E. "Eddie" White, she was very involved in the effort. Rose taught English, Spanish, and math in Vaughn and Santa Rosa. In 1923, when she married White and moved to Portales, few knew much about the early history of Roosevelt County. Rose was fascinated with the stories of the early settlers. Her interest grew as she spoke with old-timers. Rose became passionate about the area's history and initiated more formal interviews. She expanded her research to include several early-day cowboys and settlers. Some would visit at her home for several days while she recorded their memories. Rose wrote articles about the early history of the region. She assisted T. M. Pearce in research for *New Mexico Place Names*. Rose was one of the founders of the Pioneer Association of Roosevelt County and was its president and secretary for many years. (1894–1969). New Mexico Historic Women Marker Initiative.

Whitehorse, Emmi. Navajo painter and printmaker. Emmi Whitehorse is a member of the Navajo Nation who grew up speaking only the language of her people. She is a painter and print maker with degrees in fine arts from the University of New Mexico. In an interview for *Messengers of the Wind*, Whitehorse reflected on her metamorphosis from tending her family's sheep to becoming a postmodern painter and reflected on the importance of her culture, especially the role of women. "I'm interested in the presence of the woman. I'm intrigued by the femininity of the female form." She blames early Christian missionaries for disrupting traditional Navajo lifestyles and throwing "everything asunder." Whitehorse attributes her image of women as a positive force to the Navajo legend of Changing Woman. "In my family, the women ran everything." (1957–). *Messengers of the Wind.*

Clara Belle Williams. UA02040092, Hobson-Huntsinger. University Archives Photograph Collection, New Mexico State University Library Archives and Special Collections.

Williams, Clara Belle. She beat the odds. The daughter of Texas sharecroppers, Clara Belle Williams is believed to have been the first African-American graduate of New Mexico A&M College (now New Mexico State University) with a degree in English in 1937. In doing so, she defied the rules. Some reports say that, when some of her professors would not allow her in their classrooms, she took notes from the hallway. Despite these obstacles, after earning her degree, Williams taught for nearly thirty years in the Las Cruces public schools. Somehow, she and her husband, Jasper, also a teacher, found time to operate a drugstore and to farm six hundred acres. Williams's mantra was: "Get your education and make something of yourselves." Clara Belle Williams Hall is named for her at her alma mater. (1885–1994). blackprograms.nmsu/clara-belle-williams. *Notable New Mexico Women.* Collections UA02040092, Hobson-Huntsinger. University Archives. New Mexico State University Library Archives and Special Collections.

Williams, Eleanor McClintock. Daughter of privilege, rancher by choice. Born into wealth in the East, Eleanor McClintock Williams eschewed that lifestyle, preferring instead to ranch in New Mexico. Williams moved West after stints as a champion trick rider on the rodeo circuit and with Ringling Brothers and Barnum & Bailey Circus. Eleanor survived two bad marriages and successfully weathered the economic storms of the Great Depression and World War II to preserve her Rising Sun Ranch near Quemado. "We are given the strength to struggle and endure," she believed. Eleanor ran for the New Mexico Senate, became a published author, and was an accomplished artist. She was a member of the National Cowgirl Hall of Fame. Williams displayed perseverance and strength, a shining example to women everywhere. (1906–1979). West/portfolios/West.

Rose Williams.

Williams, Rose. Matriarch of Navajo pottery. Rose Williams is considered the matriarch of modern Navajo pottery. Rose learned from her aunt Grace Barlow and passed her knowledge and experience on to her daughters and others. Not all Navajo potters trace their lineage to Rose but many do. Many are close relatives. Unlike Puebloan potters, Navajo potters do not grind up old pot shards and use them for temper in creating new pottery. Navajo religion holds that the shards are filled with the spirits of their people's ancestors and forbids their reuse. Similarly, Navajo religion limits Navajo potters to using primarily Navajo carpet designs in the decoration of their pots. Rose learned very little English (many Navajo never learn English, speaking Navajo and some Spanish all their lives). She lived in a small frame house and almost never left home. Rose became a recognized potter on the reservation early and made a lot of ceremonial pottery early in her career. (1915–2015).

Wilson, Grace Barker. A bygone breed. In the summer of 1889, baby Grace Barker, just six months old, endured the long trek from Texas to New Mexico's Sapello Valley north of Las Vegas. She did so in a homemade cradle on the front seat of a covered wagon driven by her parents. That difficult beginning instilled in Grace an indomitable spirit, a zest for life, and a love for her new homeland. Following rural elementary schooling, Grace enrolled at New Mexico Normal School (now Highlands University). At age nineteen, she left, lacking a degree but with a desire to teach. Her first assignment was at Tucumcari in a flimsy one-room, frame affair set on props on the wrong side of the tracks. Thirty pupils were packed into a room supplied only with chalk, erasers, and children. Grace did her own janitorial work, built the fire each morning in a coal stove, and taught—all for $65 a month. In one early March, an unusually high windstorm blew her classroom off its props, thus ending Grace's first year of teaching. In another school in which Grace taught, there was no electricity, only homemade benches, and a hand pump, which remained frozen most of the winter. Grace endured all this and taught for another thirty-nine years. She remained in love with education "to enable success and contribute to society." After retirement, Grace published five books of poetry. At age eighty-seven Grace gave twenty-two lectures on patriotism and at age ninety-eight spoke on "Know Your New Mexico." (1889–1989). https://aauw-nm.aauw.net/files/2013/06/Grace-Barker-Wilson-Bio.pdf. *Women in Education: New Mexico.*

Dorothy Woodward. MSS 303 Box 1 Folder 82. Center for Southwest Research and Special Collections, University of New Mexico.

Woodward, Dorothy, PhD. Southwestern and Latin America scholar. Dorothy Woodward earned her doctorate from Yale University based on research into the social history of New Mexico's Spanish-speaking people. After teaching at the University of New Mexico, Woodward joined its Board of Regents. During World War II, she joined the Women's Army Corps as a private despite her advanced academic credentials. Woodward wrote numerous articles and reviews, including several on the Penitentes, as well as an interview in Mexico with Leon Trotsky. (1895–1961). *Notable New Mexico Women.*

Helene Valeska Billing Wurlitzer. Courtesy of the Helene Wurlitzer Foundation of New Mexico.

Wurlitzer, Helene Valeska Billing (V.B.). A welcome beacon for artists. Helene V. B. Wurlitzer established a foundation in Taos in 1954 to benefit artists from diverse artistic disciplines through a residency program to allow them to pursue their creative interests. Helene's presence in the art colony went unnoticed by many Taoseños. Nevertheless, her impact from the 1940s, when she became a permanent part-time resident, was substantial and lasting. Helene began buying works by Taos artists, lasting through the 1950s when she established the residency program. There were many reasons for Helene's presence in New Mexico, her interest in supporting its artists, and why she was able to do so. By 1887, Helene's father had become the foremost authority on mining in the Southwest, where he lived with his family. He also had become prosperous enough to move them back to Cincinnati, where his and his wife's families had lived since the mid-1800s. He soon decided to provide his children with Europe's cultural and educational opportunities and moved everyone to his native Germany. When her father died in 1890, Helene's mother returned with the children to Cincinnati. Helene became an astute businesswoman, continuing to manage her father's mine from Cincinnati and traveling to New Mexico to inspect it and look after the miners' welfare. In the early 1890s, she met Howard Wurlitzer, whose family manufactured the famous Wurlitzer musical instruments. They were married in 1895. While Howard ran the business, Helene continued her intellectual and artistic pursuits. After her husband died in 1928, then her mother in 1939, Helene realized little remained to hold her in Cincinnati. Beginning in 1940, Helene visited and then lived in Taos. In 1956, she made Taos her year-round home. (1874–1963). Courtesy of Wurlitzer Foundation of New Mexico.

Meskee Yanabah Yatsayte.

Yatsayte, Meskee Yanabah. A voice for a silent epidemic. Meskee Yanabah Yatsayte founded the Navajo Nation Missing Persons Updates to assist families in finding missing loved ones. "Once a person goes missing," Yatsayte says, "I always tell them, be aware that you become the advocate. You also become the investigator." She claims that no one knows the status of investigations of missing persons either on the Navajo Reservation or nationwide. "These cases are not taken seriously. They don't hit headline news." When Yatsayte began her work, she realized that Navajo people did not have a place to report missing people. Her organization's goals are spreading awareness and helping families get their voices heard, because "this is a silent epidemic." Yatsayte says that she has been scared for most of her life "because I was told not to speak. But now I have the voice, and I'm not scared anymore. And I will do this for the people that are not able to speak now." (birthdate unavailable).

WITH APPRECIATION

Writing the acknowledgements for a book is the most pleasant task. It is easy to call up the names and contributions of those who have remained with you as a writer throughout a project and who have rendered important support in many ways. It is no surprise to anyone who knows anything about this project that I begin with Barbara Bradford Taylor, EdD, the "mother" of this book. Barbara is an ardent advocate of the rightful recognition for women and is particularly proud of my choice of topic. In addition to suggesting the topic, she introduced me to Malcolm Forbes's *Women Who Made a Difference*, the model for this book, and loaned me her copy of Lori Arviso Alvord's *The Scalpel and the Silver Bear: The First Navajo Woman Surgeon Combines Western Medicine and Traditional Healing,* the first book I read upon beginning this project. And, as if that were not enough, Barbara volunteered for the thankless job of reading the manuscript in an early draft! A last-minute invaluable assist was from longtime friend Dave Wilson, who pitched in from Oregon to provide much-needed professional assistance with getting the book's photos into the desired format. When Dave became ill, George Austin took over. A true test of friendship is the last-minute correcting of electronic citations, which came from Ron George in far-off Corpus Christi and from Javier Marrufo of the Silver City Public Library, and then final edit by longtime friends Charlie McKee and Steve Fox. What eyes they possess! What copying editing skills. The book is much better than it would have been because of her sharp eye and professional attention, and I am deeply indebted to her. I cannot say enough about her expertise, not to mention the quiet encouragement. And lastly and sadly no longer here to see the final effort is my longtime teacher, mentor, editor, and friend Wayne Gunn. I hope I have heeded his stricture to make my writing fluid and smooth.

Other thanks are due to Western New Mexico University's Miller

Library, particularly Andrea Jaquez, and the Silver City Public Library, especially Donna Foley, as well as to most excellent Silver City researchers Tom Hester and "Doc" Campbell. Longtime favorite New Mexico historian Richard Melzer was an early sounding board and supporter. His ready enthusiasm influenced me to go forward. Jim Smith of Sunstone Press was on board from the beginning and graciously shared hard-to-find copies of needed books from his own library. He also suggested several other deserving subjects. Their inclusion adds to the depth of the book. My appreciation also goes to Phil and Roseanne Roberts Archulleta, authors of *Women Marked for History,* and to Beverly Duran and the women who brought to life the most important New Mexico Historic Women Marker Initiative. I haven't seen all of them, but doing so would be a great addition to anyone's New Mexico bucket list. And I thank Gretchen Brock of the New Mexico Historic Preservation Division for graciously sharing information about women remembered on the state's highway markers who are not included in the marker initiative.

As always, my thanks go to Chris Geherin of the Center for Southwest Research and Special Collections at the University of New Mexico and to Teri Reynoso of Special Collections at the Albuquerque-Bernalillo County Public Library for early encouragement and help. My gratitude also to Susan Berry, Director Emeritus of the Silver City Museum: What she knows and is willing to share without stint of Silver City history is truly astonishing. Thanks also to Chellee Chase, conformity cop on publications guidelines. And I thank the numerous women along the way with whom I discussed this project and who expressed admiration for the idea and a willingness to buy the book when it was completed. It is, and I hope they do.

For the heroic women of twentieth century New Mexico whose lives, loves, and legacies are detailed herein, I hope the few words about them have done them justice. They have been my *raison d'être* for the past couple of years. While I have may not have liked them individually each and every one, I certainly admire them collectively. New Mexico is richer for their presence. I have been so impressed with what they did and how they did it. My admiration for them is as boundless as are their ambitions and achievements. I hope I have not omitted too many who offered help; to them I offer apologies in advance.

And finally and most affectionately to my wife Peggy: She endured the birthing of yet another of my books. Pretty heroic woman herself.

BIBLIOGRAPHY AND WORKS CONSULTED

Archulleta, Phil T. and Roseanne Roberts Archulleta. *Women Marked for History: New Mexico's Women Leaders in Community and Government, Education, Military, Business, Healing Arts And Medicine, Entertainment, Cultural Preservation and the Arts*. Sunstone Press, 2013.

Albuquerque Journal. "Obituary of Yvonne Kueffer Lucero," December 2, 2018.

Alter, Judy. *Extraordinary Women of the American West*. Children's Press, Division of Grolier Publishing, 1999.

Alvord, Lori Arviso and Elizabeth Cohen Van Pelt. *The Scalpel and the Silver Bear: The First Navajo Woman Surgeon Combines Western Medicine and Traditional Healing*. Bantam Books, 1999.

And They Will Inherit It: NPR It. and-they-will-inherit-it. https://www.npr.org/2019/04/30/718794620 https://www.npr.org/2019/04/30/718794620/and-they-will-inherit-it

Anderson, Martha Shipman, ed. *Out of the Shadows: The Women of Southern New Mexico*. Rio Grande Books and New Mexico State University Library, 2012.

Armstrong, Ruth W. *Cycle of Seasons in Corrales*. Sunstone Press, 1988.

Associated Press. "Concha Ortiz y Pino de Kleven, a proponent of Hispanic culture and a former New Mexico state legislator, died here on Sept. 30." Santa Fe. October 8, 2006.

Augustine, Katherine Acoya. *Growing Up and Looking Out: My Life from Laguna Pueblo* to *Albuquerque and Tales My Grandmother Told Me and Being Laguna.* Sunstone Press, 2017.

Austin, Mary. *Earth Horizons.* New Edition, Sunstone Press, 2007.

———. *The Land of Journey's Ending.* New Edition, Sunstone Press, 2007.

Babcock, Barbara A. and Nancy J. Parazeo. *Daughters of the Desert: Women Anthropologists and the Native American Southwest, 1880-1980.* University of New Mexico Press, 1988.

Babcock, Barbara A. and Guy and Doris Monthan. *The Pueblo Storyteller.* University of Arizona Press, 1988.

Bachrach, Arthur J., Nita Murphy and Judith Nasse. *A Life in Full: Millicent Rogers.* ABQ Press, 2012.

Baker, Deborah. "Lala Was New Mexico's 1st Female Governor" *Albuquerque Journal,* October 24, 2010.

Benson, Nancy C. *Notable New Mexico Women: A Selected Index.* American Association of University Women, Albuquerque Branch, 1976.

Berry, Susan. "Coloring Outside the Lines: Empowered women in territorial and early-statehood Silver City." *Desert Exposure,* March 2012.

Bills, Garland D. *Sadie Orchard: Madam of New Mexico's Black Range.* Hillsboro Historical Society, 2019.

Birchell, Donna Blake. *Wicked Women of New Mexico.* The History Press, 2014.

Bird, Sarah. *Daughter of a Daughter of a Queen: A Novel.* St. Martin's Press, 2018.

Blair, Mary Ellen. *A Life Well Led: The Biography of Barbara Freire-Marreco*

Aitken, British Anthropologist. Sunstone Press, 2008.

Bullis, Don. *New Mexico Historical Biographies*. Rio Grande Books, 2011.

———. *New Mexico: A Biographical Dictionary 1540-1980 Volume I*. Rio Grande Books, 2007.

———. Bullis, Don. *New Mexico: A Biographical Dictionary 1540-1980 Volume II*. Rio Grande Books, 2008.

Burns, Patrick, ed. *In the Shadow of Los Alamos: Selected Writings of Edith Warner*. Expanded Edition. University of New Mexico Press, 2001.

Cather, Willa. *Death Comes for the Archbishop*. Alfred A. Knopf, 1927.

Chávez, Denise. *A Taco Testimony: Meditations on Family, Food and Culture*. Rio Nuevo Publishers, 2006.

Chegin, Rita Kasch. *Survivors: Women of the Southwest*. Yucca Tree Press, 1991.

Church, Peggy Pond. Shelley Armitage Ed. *Wind's Trail: The Early Life of Mary Austin*. Museum of New Mexico Press, 1990.

———. *The House at Otowi Bridge: The Story of Edith Warner and Los Alamos*. University of New Mexico Press, 1988.

Cleaveland, Agnes Morley. *No Life for a Lady*. Houghton Mifflin, 1941.

Cohen, Leslie. "Dutton's Dirty Diggers: 'She Taught Us to be Bold.'" *El Palacio,* 111 (Summer 2006): 34-37.

Colby, Catherine. *Kate Chapmen: Adobe Builder in 1930s Santa Fe*. Sunstone Press, 2012.

Coulich, Bernice. "A Congresswoman Out of the West." *The New York Times*, 22 October, 1933.

Cuba, Stanley L. *Olive Rush: A Hoosier Artist in New Mexico*. Minnetrista Cultural Foundation, 1992.

Dabney, Thomas Ewing. “Background for a Book.” *New Mexico Magazine* (July 24, 1946,): 49-52.

Davis, Cynthia and Verner D. Mitchell, eds. *Western Echoes of the Harlem Renaissance: The Life and Writings of Anita Scott Coleman*. University of Oklahoma Press, 2008.

Dawkins, Cecil, ed. *A Woman of the Century: Frances Minerva Nunnery (1898-1997). Her Story in Her Own Memorable Voice as Told to Cecil Dawkins*. University of New Mexico Press, 2002.

Deacon, Desley. *Elsie Clews Parsons: Inventing Modern Life*. The University of Chicago Press, 1997.

Devereaux, Jan. *Pistols, Petticoats & Poker. The Real Lottie Deno: No Lies or Alibis*. High-Lonesome Books, 2009.

Dietrich, Margetta Stewart. Sylvia Loomis, ed. *New Mexico Recollections, Part I*. Vergara Printing Company, Santa Fe,, 1959.

———. *New Mexico Recollections, Part II*. Vergara Printing Company, 1961.

Elliott, Erica M. *Medicine and Miracles in the High Desert: My Life Among the Navajo People*. Balboa Press, 2019.

Eisenstadt, Pauline. *A Woman in Both Houses: My Career in New Mexico Politics*. University of New Mexico Press, 2012.

Evans, Max. *Madam Millie: Bordellos from Silver City to Ketchikan*. University of New Mexico Press, 2002.

Feinstein, Elaine. *Lawrence and His Women: The Intimate Life of D.H. Lawrence*. HarperCollins, 1993.

Fergusson, Erna. *Dancing Gods: Indian Ceremonials of New Mexico and Arizona*. Alfred A. Knopf, 1931.

Fitzpatrick, George, ed. *This is New Mexico*. Horn & Wallace, 1948.

Forbes, Malcolm S. and Jeff Bloch. *Women Who Made a Difference: One hundred fascinating tales of unsung heroines & little-known stories of famous women who changed their world & ours*. Simon and Schuster, 1990.

Foote, Cheryl J. *Women of the New Mexico Frontier 1846-1912*. University of New Mexico Press, 2005.

Fox, Stephen. Unpublished essay on Annette Kinyon, 2019.

Gilbert Cabeza de Baca, Fabiola. *We Fed Them Cactus*. University of New Mexico Press, 1954.

Gilbert, Fabiola C. *Historic Cookery*. Ancient City Press, 1970.

Gilmore, Jann Haynes. *Olive Rush: Finding Her Place in the Santa Fe Art Colony*. Museum of New Mexico Press, 2016.

Georgi-Findlay, Brigitte. *The Frontiers of Women's Writing: Women's Narratives and the Rhetoric of Westward Expansion*. University of Arizona Press, 1996.

Gilpin, Laura. *The Enduring Navaho*. University of Texas Press, 1968.

———. *The Pueblos; A Camera Chronicle*. Hastings House, 1941.

"Grant County feels influence of progressive business women. Hold Important Places as Heads of Large Commercial Organizations, in Business and Education, Women are Helping." *Silver City Enterprise* (March 12, 1920).

Glasrud, Bruce A. Ed. *African American History in New Mexico: Portraits from Five Hundred Years*. University of New Mexico Press, 2013.

Grattan, Virginia. *Mary Colter: Builder Upon the Red Earth*. Northland Press, 1980.

Greenway, Phaedra. *Beside the Rio Hondo: A Memoir of Rural New Mexico*. Sunstone Press, 2007.

Hall, Ruth K. *A Place of Her Own: The Story of Elizabeth Garrett*. Sunstone Press, 1983.

Hamm, Ron. "Susan Parks: An Unlikely Heroine." *True West*. (October. 1982).

———. *Ross Calvin: Interpreter of the Southwest*. Sunstone Press, Santa Fe, 2016.

Hanners, LaVerne. *Girl on a Pony*. University of Oklahoma Press, 1994.

Henderson, Eva Pendleton. *Wild Horse in My Blood: An 1890s Girlhood in New Mexico*. Sunstone Press, 2001.

Hillerman, Tony. Ed. *The Spell of New Mexico*. University of New Mexico Press, 1984.

Hmura, Merideth A. *Mountain View Ranch: 1915-1945 George A. and Mattie R. Viles*. Leaning Pine Publishing, 1996.

Houghton, Howard. Jacobs, Margaret D. "Clara True and Female Moral Authority" *The Human Tradition in the American West. Faculty Publications*, Department of History. 24. http://digitalcommons.unl.edu/historyfacpub/24. Published in *The Human Tradition in the American West.* Tong, Benson and Regan A. Lutz Eds. SR Books, 2002.

Jacobs, Margaret D. "Making Savages of Us All: White Women, Pueblo Indians, and the Controversy over Indian Dances in the 1920s." *Faculty Publications, Department of History*, 17. http://digitalcommons.unl.edu/historyfacpub/.

Jamison, Cheryl Alters and Bill Jamison. "Recipes from the Hope Chest: Our shared food traditions are part of what make us all New Mexicans." *New Mexico Magazine*. (February 2013).

Jaramillo, Cleofas M. *Romance of a Little Village Girl.* University of New Mexico 2000.

Jewell, Andrew and Janis Stout, eds. *The Selected Letters of Willa Cather.* Alfred A. Knopf, 2013.

Jones, Rachel. "Inside Deb Haaland's Historic Bid to Become One of First Native American Congresswomen." *National Geographic (* November 7, 2018.)

Katz, Jane, ed. *Messengers of the Wind: Native American Women Tell Their Life Stories*. Ballantine Books, 1995.

Kalloch, Eunice and Ruth K. Hall. *The First Ladies of New Mexico*. The Lighting Tree, 1982.

King, Patsy Crow. *Sadie Orchard (The Time of Her Life).* PDX Printing, 2008.

Kofalk, Harriet. *No Woman Tenderfoot: Florence Merriam Bailey, Pioneer Naturalist*. Texas A&M University Press, 1989.

Lane, Lydia Spencer. *I Married a Soldier*. University of New Mexico Press, 1988.

Latimar, Rosa Walston. *Harvey Houses of New Mexico: Historic Hospitality from Raton to Deming*. History Press, 2015.

"Leeches [*sic*] Will Produce Radium Concentrate By New Process." *Silver City Enterprise* (February 2, 1923).

Levin, Jennifer. "Stories of the Forgotten: Susan Hudson." *Paseotiempo, Santa Fe New Mexican*. (August 17 2018).

Lippard, Lucy L. *Down Country: The Tano of the Galisteo Basin, 1250-1782*. Museum of New Mexico Press, 2010.

Lippard, Lucy R. *Undermining: A Wild Ride Through Land Use, Politics, and Art in the Changing West.* The New Press, 2014.

Lippard, Lucy R. "Walking the Tightrope" With Enrique Lamadrid, Ramon Gutierrez, and Miguel A. Gandert. In *New Mexico Profundo: Rituals of an Indo-Hispano Homeland*. Museum of New Mexico Press and National Hispanic Cultural Center of New Mexico, 2000.

Loveless, Joan Potter. *Three Weavers*. University of New Mexico Press, 1982.

Luhan, Mabel Dodge. *Edge of Taos Desert: An Escape to Reality.* University of New Mexico Press, 1965.

———. *Winter in Taos.* (Facsimile of the Original 1935 Edition Harcourt, Brace). Sunstone Press, 2007.

Lynes, Barbara Buhler and Ann Paden, eds. *Maria Chabot—Georgia O'Keefe. Correspondence–1941–1949*. University of New Mexico Press and Georgia O'Keefe Museum, 2003.

Magoffin, Susan Shelby. *Down the Santa Fe Trail and Into Mexico, the Diary of Susan Shelby Magoffin, 1846-1847*. Stella M. Drumm, ed. University of Nebraska Press, 1982.

Marah, Bertie Stroup. *Rusty Spoon to Silver: An Artist's Memoir*. Sunstone Press, 2012.

"Margaret Armer-Reid-Woman ahead of her time." Newsletter of the Hillsboro Historical Society, Vol. 7, No. 2, (May 2014).

Marriott, Alice. *Maria: The Potter of San Ildefonso*. University of Oklahoma Press, 1948.

Mary C. Wheelwright Autobiography and Related Materials, Center for Southwest Research and Special Collections, University Libraries, University of New Mexico.

McKellen, Ian, Janet Suzman, Ava Gardner, Penelope Keith, and John Gielgud. *Priest of Love*. New York: Christopher Miles, Kino Lorber. 1981.

Martin, Henry. *Agnes Martin: Pioneer, Painter, Icon*. Schaffner Press, 2018.

Martin, Katherine. *Women of Courage: Inspiring Stories from the Women Who Lived Them*. New World Library, 1999.

Melzer, Richard. *Buried Treasures: Famous and Unusual Gravesites in New Mexico History* Sunstone Press, 2007.

———. *Fred Harvey Houses of the Southwest*. Arcadia Publishing, 2008.

Meyer, Marian. *Mary Donoho: New First Lady of the Santa Fe Trail*. Ancient City Press, 1991.

Miller, Kristie. *Isabella Greenway: An Enterprising Woman*. University of Arizona Press.

Miller, Darlis A. *Open Range: The Life of Agnes Morley Cleaveland*. University of Oklahoma Press, 2010.

Mock, Charlotte K. *Bridges: New Mexico Black Women 1900-1950*, New Mexico Commission on the Status of Women, 1985.

———. "African American Women in New Mexico," in *History of Hope: The African American Experience in New Mexico*. Albuquerque Museum, 1996.

Morrill, Claire. *A Taos Mosaic: Portrait of a New Mexico Village*. University of New Mexico Press, 1973.

Morris, James McGrath. "The Taste for Chile: The Original New Mexico Cookery." Pasotiempo, *Santa Fe New Mexican (* September 1, 2017).

Morris, Juddi. *The Harvey Girls: Women Who Civilized the West*. Walker & Co., 1994.

Myers, Joan. *Pie Town Woman*. University of New Mexico Press, 2001.

Niederman, Sharon. *A Quilt of Words: Women's Diaries, Letters & Original Accounts of Life in the Southwest, 1860-1960*. Johnson Books, 1988.

Nichols, Edith M. Bowyer. *Observations of a Ranch Woman in New Mexico*. Editor Publishing, 1901. (Pranava Books, India).

New Mexico Historic Women Marker Initiative. Funded by 2007 Legislature. Beverly Duran, Chair. Santa Fe.

New Mexico Historic-Scenic Markers, New Mexico Historic Preservation Division, State of New Mexico. Gretchen Brock, historian, Santa Fe. Ongoing.

New Mexico Women Legislators Since Statehood. New Mexico Legislative Council Services, 1995.

Newcomb, Franc Johnson. *Navajo Neighbors*. University of Oklahoma Press, 1966.

Ortego y Gasca, Felipe de. "Afro-Hispanic Writer Anita Scott Coleman and the Harlem Renaissance West." Amazon.com. (November 18, 2015).

Marriot, Alice. *These Are the People: Some Notes On the Southwestern Indians*. Laboratory of Anthropology, 1949.

Nelson, Kate. *Helen Hardin: A Straight Line Curved.* Little Standing Spruce Publishing, 2012.

Nelson, Mary Carol. *Pablita Velarde: The Story of an American Indian.* Dillion Press, 1971.

100 Years of Filmmaking in New Mexico. New Mexico Magazine and New Mexico Film Office, 1998.

Petrick, Neila Skinner. Illustrator Daggi Wallace. *Katherine Skinner Otero: High Flyer*. Pelican Publishing, 2006.

Poling-Kempes, Lesley. *Ladies of the Canyons*. University of Arizona Press, 2015.

———. *Valley of Shining Stone: The Story of Abiquiu*. University of Arizona Press, 1997.

———. *The Harvey Girls: Women Who Opened the West*. Paragon House, 1991.

Pollitzer, Anita. *A Woman on Paper: Georgia O'Keeffe. The Letters & Memoir of a Legendary Friendship*. Touchstone. 1988.

Pope, Neta and Andrea Jaquez. *The Fort Bayard Story, 1866-1899: The Soldiers... The Hostile Apache Indians... The Settlers in Harm's* Way. Published by the authors, 2011.

Powell, Lawrence Clark. *Southwest Classics: The Creative Literature of the Arid Lands. Essays on the Books and Their Writers*. Ward Ritchie Press, 1973.

"Radium ores at White Signal. Mineral Torbernite discovered by Mr. and Mrs. A.A. Leach." *Silver City Enterprise (* March 12, 1920).

Reed, Maureen. A *Woman's Place: Women Writing New Mexico*. University of New Mexico Press, 2005.

Reily, Nancy Hopkins. *Georgia O'Keeffe: A Private Friendship. Part I. Walking the Sun Prairie Land*. Sunstone Press, 2007.

Richter, Conrad. *The Sea of Grass*. Alfred A. Knopf, 1971.

Richardson, Barbara J. and Euola J. Cox. *Noteworthy Black Women of New Mexico: Past and Present*. Publisher not identified. 1977.

Riley, Glenda and Richard W. Etulain, eds. *By Grit & Grace: Eleven Women Who Shaped the American West*. Fulcrum Publishing, 1997.

Roberts, Kathaleen. "Etched in Time: Taos artist Gene Kloss created a legacy in light and dark." *Albuquerque Journal*. (November 25, 2018).

Robertson, Edna and Sarah Nestor. *Artists of the Canyons and Caminos: Santa Fe, the Early Years.* Ancient City Press, 1976.

"Rocky Trail is new gold camp. Woman credited with discovery of richest ore found in recent years." *Silver City Enterprise*, May 30, 1919.

Rose, Cynthia. *Lottie Deno: Gambling Queen of Hearts*. Clear Light Publishers, 1994.

Rudnick, Lois Palken. *Mabel Dodge Luhan: New Woman, New Worlds*. University of New Mexico Press, 1984.

———. "Mabel Dodge Luhan and New Mexico's Anglo Arts Community." *New Mexico Lives: Profiles and Historical Stories*. Richard W. Etulain, ed. University of New Mexico Press, 2002.

Russell, Marian Sloan. *Land of Enchantment: Memoirs of Marian Russell Along the Santa Fe Trail as dictated to Mrs. Hal Russell.* University of New Mexico Press, 1981.

Samora, Vangi, ed. *Mujeres Valerosas…meet the extraordinary women of the Hispanic Women's Council.* Hispanic Women's Council., 2006.

Sanchez, Lynda A. *Eve Ball, Woman Among Men: A Photo Essay*. Lincoln County Historical Society, 2007.

———. "Stories of Survival as told by Eve Ball." *La Crónica de Nuevo México*. Issue Number 81 (October 2009).

Sanders, Gordon E. *Oscar E. Berninghaus: Master Painter of American Indians and the Frontier West*. Taos Heritage Publishing Company, 1985.

Sandweiss, Martha, ed. *Denizens of the Desert: A Tale in Words and Pictures of Life Among the Navaho Indians. The Letters of Elizabeth W. Forster/ Photographs by Laura Gilpin*. University of New Mexico Press, 1988.

Scott, Jay. *Changing Woman: The Life and Art of Helen Hardin*. Northland Press, 1989.

Segale, Blandina. *At the End of the Santa Fe Trail*. Bruce Publishing Company, 1948.

Silko, Leslie Marmon. *The Turquoise Ledge*. Viking, 2010.

———. *Yellow Woman and a Beauty of the Spirit: Essays on Native American Life Today*. Simon & Schuster, 1996.

Smith, Craig. *Sing My Whole Life Long: Jenny Vincent's Life in Folk Music and Activism*. University of New Mexico Press, 2007.

Sparks, Twana. "The Queen of Brewer Hill: Remembering Madame Rebecca Brewer, healer, philanthropist, spiritualist, hill namesake and Silver City character." *Desert Exposure*, (September 2013).

Straw, Mary J. *Loretto: The Sisters and Their Santa Fe Chapel*. West America Publishing, 1983.

Tilchen, Maida. *Land Beyond Maps*. Savvy Press, 2009.

"The Story of Isabella Greenway And How Roosevelt Paths Have Always Crossed Those of the Arizona Congresswoman." *The New York Times* (December 8, 1933).

Thomas, D. H. *The Southwestern Indian Detours: The story of the Fred Harvey/Santa Fe Railway experiment in 'detourism.'* Hunter Publishing, 1978.

Three Wise Women: The Life and Legacy of Eva and the Leonoras. Women's International Study Center, 2018.

Vaccariello, Linda. "Sister Blandina and the Road to Sainthood." *Cincinnati Magazine (*April 2, 2016).

Velarde, Pablita. *Old Father Story Teller*. Clear Light Publishers, 1989.

Wallace, Susan Arnold Elston. *The Land of the Pueblos*. John B. Alden, 1888.

Waters, Frank. *The Woman at Otowi Crossing*. Alan Swallow, 1966.

Warren, Nina-Otero. *Old Spain in Our Southwest*. Facsimile of the Original 1936 Edition Harcourt, Brace. Sunstone Press, 2006.

West, Beverly. *More Than Petticoats: Remarkable New Mexico Women*. Globe Pequot Press, 2001.

Weigle, Marta, ed. *Women of New Mexico: Depression Era Images*. Ancient City Press, 1993.

Weigle, Marta and Kyle Fiore. *Santa Fe & Taos: The Writer's Era 1916-1941*. Ancient City Press, 1994.

Weigle, Marta. "Pie Town: A slice of homestead life." *New Mexico Magazine* November 1996. 22, 28-31.

Whitney and Josephine Koogler. *Women in Education: New Mexico*. Nortex Press, 1977.

Woods, Betty. *101 Men and Women of New Mexico: 101 Men and Women Who Contributed to New Mexico's History*. Sunstone Press, 1976.

SUBJECTS BY FIELD

Activism and Suffrage. Paula Gunn Allen, Mary Elizabeth Egan Arango, Julia Brown Asplund, Alice McLellan Birney, Ella Boyer, Mela Sedillo Brewster, Perlina Cassidy, Mary Lea Chabot, Marjorie Bell Chambers, Kate Chapman, Judy Chicago, Dorothy Cline, Amber Kanazbah Crotty, Adrienne Dare, Margretta Dietrich, Christine Eber, Fabiola Cabeza de Baca Gilbert, Isabella Greenway, Judith Harris, LaDonna Harris, Tura Hawk, Pearl Foster Hicks, Alice Hoppes, The Howells, Fannye Irving-Gibbs, Cleofas Martinez Jaramillo, Debbie Jaramillo, Eunice Kalloch, Pearl Foster Hicks, Annette Kinyon, Kleven, Concha Ortiz y Pino, Pearl Foster Hicks, Ruth Laughlin, Frances Lee, Lucy Lippard, Mabel Dodge Luhan, Demetria Martinez, Trinidad Medina, Nellie Moore, Graciela Olivárez, "Nina" Maria Adelina Emilia Otero-Warren, Jenny Ramo, Barbara Richardson, Claudine Riddle, Lucy Salazar, Salt of the Earth Sisterhood, Allyson Siwik, Maria Gutiérrez Spencer, Clara True, Jenny Vincent, Elizabeth Warren, Meskee Yanabah Yatsayte.

Arts and Music. Florence Dibell Bartlett, Sallie Bingham, E. Boyd, Mela Sedillo Brewster, Regina Albarado Cata, Perlina Cassidy, Kate Chapman, Judy Chicago, Mary Elizabeth Jane Colter, Helen Quintana Cordero, Leonora Curtin, Natalie Curtis, Elizabeth Willis DeHuff, Cora Durand, Grace Keene Edmister, Estella Garcia, Laura Gilpin, Glenna Maxey Goodacre, Blanche Grant, Virginia Gutierrez, Helen Hardin, Mary Hestia, Susan Hudson, Henriette Hurd, Cleofas Martinez Jaramillo, Alice Klauber, Gene Kloss, Dorothy Dunn Kramer, Gertrude Prokosch Kurath, Joan Potter Loveless, Merina Lujan Pop Challe (Blue Flower), Mabry Agnes

Martin, Agueda Martinez, Maria Antonia Montoya Martinez "Povika" (Flower Leaf) or "Poveka" (Pond Lily), Ramita Simbola Maria Martinez (Summer Harvest), Edwina Milner, Natachee Scott Momaday, Dorothy Morang, Georgia O'Keeffe, Florence Miller Pierce, Tonita Peña, Qyah Ah, Agnew Lawrence Pelton, Virginia Roediger, Susan Rothenberg, Virginia T. Romero, Olive Rush, Eugenie Shonnard, Agi Sims, Eva Springer, Dorothy Stewart, Margarita Maria Tafoya, Corn Blossom, Daisy Taugelchee, Juanita T. Toledo, Pha-Wa-Luh-Luh (Ring-Cloud Around the Moon), Pablita Velarde, Tse Tsan. (Golden Dawn), Evelyn M. Vigil, Un-Pha-Kee (Young Doe), Jenny Vincent, Vera Von Blumenthal, Mary Cabot Wheelwright, Amelia Elizabeth White, Emmi Whitehorse, Dorothea Marie Fricke Whitecraft, Rose Williams.

Communications. Barbara Awalt, Frances Clingenpeel, Etha Gray, Agnes Head, Ruth Bush Jones, Mary Lynch, Demetria Martinez, Esther Martinez, P'Oe Tsawa (Blue Water), Frankie McCarty, Robin Martin, Susan Parks, Sarah J. Rooke, Annie Dodge Wauneka.

Education and Scholarship. Julia Brown Asplund, Katherine Acoya Augustine, Perlina Cassidy, Marjorie Bell Chambers, Dorothy Cline, Wilmatte Cockerell, Eula W. Cox, Adrienne Dare, Bertha Pauline Dutton, Isabel Eckles, Myrtle Attaway Farquhar, Mildred Gunn Fitzpatrick, Marion Fleck, Mary Louise Foraker, Estella Garcia, Fabiola Cabeza de Baca Gilbert, Maria Dolores Gonzales, Carol Begay Green, LaVerne Hanners, Emily Harwood, Tura Hawk, Fannye Irving-Gibbs, Ida Jackson, Margaret Kennedy, Lily Klassner, Matilda Koehler, Frances Lee, Manuelita de Atocha (Mela) Lucero Leger, Lauretta Loftus, Emily Long, Georgia Lee Lusk, Susie Rayos Marmon Ga-was goo mea (Early Riser), Esther Martinez P'Oe Tsawa (Blue Water), Natachee Scott Momaday, Bessie Moore, "Nina" Maria Mattie Parker, Jesusita Acosta Perrault, Ruth McCormick Simms, Adelina Emilia Otero-Warren, Clara Belle Williams, Grace Barker Wilson, Dorothy Woodward.

Farming and Ranching. Margaret Armer-Reid, Jacqueline J. Baca, Doris Caudill, Linda Davis, Dulcelina Salce Curtis, Carlotta and Monica Gallegos, Mollie Klapp, Frances Lee, Jesse MacMillan, Antonia Moraga, Ada McPherson Morley, Dessie Sawyer, Fern Sawyer, Eleanor Williams.

Finance and Business. Bertha Ferse Gusdorf, Matilda Koehler, Yvonne Kueffer Lucero, Harriet Belle Sammons, Clara True.

Government and Politics. Margaret Abreu, Dolores Armijo de Chavez, Maralyn Budke, Soledad Chavez de Chaćon, Marjorie Bell Chambers, Dorothy Cline, Loise Holland Coe, Diane Denish, Suzanne Huebner Dulle, Isabel Eckles, Pauline Eisenstadt, Inez Gill, Isabella Greenway, Michelle Lujan Grisham, Debra Haaland, Debbi Jaramillo, Mari-Luci Jaramillo, Myra Ellen Jenkins, Alice King, Georgia Lee Lusk, Kleven, Concha Ortiz y Pino, Patricia Madrid, Susana Martinez, Frances Neff, Lilly Neil, "Nina" Maria Adelina Emilia Otero-Warren, Dessie Sawyer, Fern Sawyer, Carrie Tingley, Annie Dodge Wauneka.

History. Evelyn (Eva) Daly, Katherine Ball, Marjorie Bell Chambers, Carol Paradise Decker, Kathy Flynn, Fannye Irving-Gibbs, Darlis Miller, Rose Powers White,

Law. Ruth L. Kovnat, Petra Jiminez Maes, Pamela Burgy Minzner, Martha Vázquez, Mary Coon Walters.

Literature. Paula Gunn Allen, Laura Adams Armer, Mary Austin, Elsa McCormick Barker, Sallie Bingham, Maude Elizabeth McFie Bloom, E. Boyd, Alice Bullock, Perlina Cassidy, Willa Cather, Dorothy Cave, Mary Lea Chabot, Chavez, Peggy Pond Church, Ann Nolan Clark, Alice Morley Cleaveland, Anita Scott Coleman, Natalie Curtis, Carol Paradise Decker, Erna Fergusson, Kathy Flynn, Fabiola Cabeza de Baca Gilbert, Laura Gilpin, Blanche Grant, LaVerne Hanners, Alice Corbin Henderson, Eva Pendleton Henderson, Dorothy Hughes, Julia Keleher, Lesley Poling-Kempes, Ruth Laughlin, Lucy Lippard, Mabel Dodge Luhan, Alice Marriott, Demetria Martinez, Darlis Miller, "Nina" Maria Adelina Emilia Otero-Warren, Dorothy Pillsbury, Sharman Russell, May Sarton, Elsie Shepley Sergeant, Julia Moss Seton, Leslie Marmon Silko, JoAnn Soge Track, Marta Weigle.

Religion. Mary Clara Alarid, Susan Carty Praxedes, Mary Dissette, Marie Katherine Drexel, Mary Louise Eldridge and Mary E. Raymond, Hendrina Hospers, Sister Vincent O'Keefe, Maria Rosa Rosister Segale (Sister Blandine), Mary Lodisa Stright.

Science and Medicine. Sister Mary Joaquin Bitler (SC), Sophie Bledsoe Brophy Aberle, Lori Arviso Alvord, Jesusita Aragon, Florence Merriam Bailey, Jeanne Banks, Ruth Benedict, Alice Blake, Meta Christy, Wilmatte Cockerell, Leonora Curtin, Natalie Curtis, Bertha Pauline Dutton, Erica Elliott, Florence Hawley Ellis, Emma Estrada, Marion Fleck, Elizabeth Forster, Evelyn Fisher Frisbie, Myrtle Greenfield, Esther Goldfrank, Elinor Gregg (RN), Jane Hall, Betty Harris, Dolores Hoffman, Lilli Hornig, Eleanor Jette, Frances Leach, Mary DeSales Leheny, Tieraona Low Dog, Mary Marshall, Dorothy McKibbin, Sister Vincent O'Keefe, Mollie Reebel, Alice Rice, Josephine Waconda, Estella Ford Warren, Margaret Washburne-Werner, Ellen Williams.

Social Sciences. Sophie Bledsoe Brophy Aberle, Barbara Freire Aitken, Ruth Benedict, Ruth Leah Bernheim Bunzel, Bertha Pauline Dutton, Christine Eber, Florence Hawley Ellis, Esther Goldfrank, Alice Marriott, Esther P'Oe Tsawa (Blue Water), Franc Newcomb, Elsie Parsons, Gladys Reichard, Anna Shepard, Mary Shepardson, Matilda Coxe Stevenson, Amelia Elizabeth White.

INDEX

Page numbers in *italics* refer to photographs or illustrations.

N

CPSIA information can be obtained
at www.ICGtesting.com
Printed in the USA
JSHW061243291222
35482JS00002B/194